How to Through Life

Dr. Donald DeMarco

How to Navigate Through Life
Copyright © 2018 by Dr. Donald DeMarco
Designed by James Kent Ridley
Published by Goodbooks Media
Printed in U.S.A.

ISBN: 9781729000687

Ad Majorem Dei Gloriam

3453 Aransas
Corpus Christi, Texas, 78411
www.goodbookmedia.com

ACKNOWLEDGEMENT

The author is grateful to The Wanderer, Human Life International, and The Catholic Register for granting permission to reproduce some of the articles contained in this book.

DEDICATION

To the memory of William Kurelek, artist, mentor, and friend.

January 1, 2018, Kitchener, Ontario

Self Portrait

"You have a man in a predicament and on the move in a real world of real things, a world which is a sacrament and a mystery; a pilgrim whose life is a searching and a finding."

Walker Percy, *Signposts in a Strange Land*

TABLE OF CONTENTS

Part One:

I Do Not Enter
- 1) The Truth about Truth 13
- 2) The Demotion of Truth 17
- 3) Escape from Cynicism 21
- 4) The Case Against the Preposterous 25
- 5) The Difficulty with Diversity 29

II Detour from Reality
- 1) Retreating from Reality 35
- 2) We Are All Equal in the Dark 39
- 3) Who Are the Barbarians? 43
- 4) Incursions and Demolitions 47
- 5) Strictly Speaking 51

III Slippery When Wet
- 1) Madness in the Workplace 57
- 2) Can Vice Be a Virtue? 61
- 3) Higher Education 63
- 4) Is Diversity a Virtue? 67
- 5) The Fetus and the Future 71

IV Poor Visibility
- 1) There Are No Human Beings 77
- 2) Plan One from Outer Space 81
- 3) Safe at Home, Out at Third 85
- 4) The Limits of Equality 89
- 5) From Debate to Mockery 93

V Fog Patches
- 1) Lead Us Not into Temptation 99

2)	Controlling My Destiny	105
3)	Brotherhood without Fatherhood	107
4)	A New Pseudo Argument for atheism	111
5)	Gray Matter	115

Part Two:

I Proceed with Caution

1)	Philosophy and the Unexamined Life	123
2)	In Principio Erat Verbum	127
3)	The Four Rights	131
4)	The Complete Thinker	135
5)	A Note of Good News	139

II Yield to Common Sense

1)	Does Common Sense Have a Future?	143
2)	Clarity in a Time of Crisis	147
3)	The Obligation to Be Intelligent	151
4)	In Defense of Duty	155
5)	Ideals and Fantasies	159

III Right of Way

1)	In Praise of Clarity	165
2)	The Importance of Placing Second	169
3)	A Modesty Proposal	173
4)	Audrey Hepburn's Beauty Tips	177
5)	Anxiety and Peace	179

IV One Way

1)	Stop and Go, but Don't Think	185
2)	The Secret of Longevity	189
3)	Philosophy's Practicality	193
4)	The Role of the Heart in Higher Education	197
5)	Play It Again, Sam	201

V Resume Speed

1) Providence 207
2) The Realism of Christianity 211
3) The Importance of Holidays 215
4) Christmas 219
5) Re-sacralizing the Sacred 221

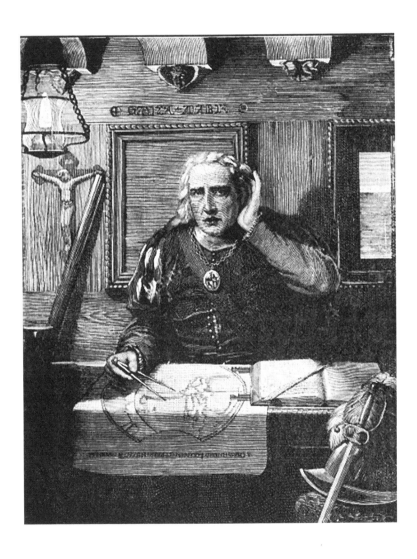

INTRODUCTION

The word "navigate" brings to mind two things. The first involves the presence of difficulties. These difficulties may be alternately described as obstacles, problems, troubles, or dangers, each of which must be overcome. Therefore, intelligence and courage are required. The second is the need for a guide that is external to the navigator. The North Star, the compass, gyroscopes, and maps have served this purpose historically. In a moral context, The Good Book has served this need very well.

In the present age, however, many prefer to go on cruise control rather than exert the effort required to navigate through life. The path of least resistance, however, leads to nowhere. Novelist John Updike spoke of the contemporary world as existing "between the death and rebirth of the gods, when there is nothing to steer by but sex and stoicism and the stars." Nonetheless, hedonistic pleasure, apathy and the stars, whether celestial or celebratory, cannot provide adequate guidance for life's journey. Yet, the current situation is not quite as bleak as the one Updike portrays.

William Kurelek's *Balsam Avenue After Heavy Snowfall*, which graces the cover of this book, illustrates how ordinary people can overcome the hardships of winter and experience community, cooperation, friendship, play, and joy. The problems their street represents are enough to fulfill their navigational needs. Madeleine Delbrêl, who has been called an "uncloistered St. Thérèse of Lisieux," has stated that "We, the ordinary people of the streets, believe with all our might that this street, this world, where God has placed us, is our place of holiness."

In his Preface to Delbrêl's *We, the Ordinary People of the Streets*, the distinguished theologian Hans Urs von Balthasar states that her writings "explore the Christians' role in a secular society, the difficulty of faith in an atheistic environment, the need for prayer, the centrality of the Church and the fundamental importance of loving both God and our neighbors." Delbrêl, a staunch atheist in her teens found a way to navigate through life by silencing her ego and heeding the signposts along the way.

The first part of this book warns against traps set by the secular world. There are places we should not enter. It behooves us to avoid unnecessary detours, to be wary of slippery road conditions, poor visibility, and fog patches. It is essential that we see things clearly. The second part advises that we proceed with caution, yield to common sense, and obtain the right of way. We may resume speed when we find the one way along which we can navigate successfully.

We are navigators, wayfarers, pilgrims, journeymen, and adventurers. The joys of a well-traveled life are well worth the effort they demand.

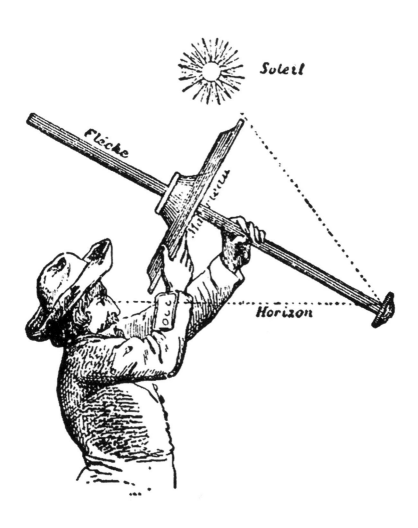

ONE

DO NOT ENTER

THE TRUTH ABOUT TRUTH

The human mind is made for truth. And truth is the natural conformity between the mind and that which is. Saint Thomas Aquinas expressed it both accurately and in his accustomed serene manner: "The human intellect is measured by things so that man's thought is not true on its own account but is called true in virtue of its conformity with things."

Nonetheless human beings often insist that truth belongs to the mind alone, severed from anything outside of itself. "Men are most anxious to find truth," wrote the esteemed philosophical historian Etienne Gilson, "but very reluctant to accept it. We do not like to be cornered by rational evidence . . . even though truth is there in its commanding objectivity. . . Finding the truth is not so hard; what is hard is not to run away from it once we have found it."

Winston Churchill, though not of the same temperament a Gilson, but of this same mind on this point, remarked that "Truth is incontrovertible. Panic may resent it, ignorance may deride it, malice may distort it, but there it is." The truth about truth, therefore, is that its acceptance requires a host of virtues, not the least of which are courage and humility, qualities that are not often possessed by the same individual. We need courage, because truth can be unpopular, difficult, and

run contrary to the party line. It requires humility to acknowledge that the truth is sourced in something other than myself, and ultimately in God.

Thus, in 1933, the Bavarian minister of education, a certain Hans Schemm, could deliver the following message to an assemblage of university professors: "From this day on, you will no longer have to examine whether something is true of not, but exclusively whether or not it corresponds to the Nazi ideology."

The courage to speak the truth, even when it is most urgently needed, is often derided. We celebrate the 100th anniversary of the birth of Alexandr Solzhenitsyn (December 11, 1918) precisely because, despite being derided, he remained faithful to the truth. In his 1970 Nobel Prize acceptance speech he quoted a Russian proverb: "One word of truth shall outweigh the whole world." This adage has certainly outlasted more than a hundred years and was consistently embodied throughout Solzhenitsyn's life. But it was in his Harvard commencement address that his courage to speak the truth reached a dramatic climax. He reminded his audience of 20,000 attendees that Harvard's motto is *Veritas* and prefaced his message by stating "truth is seldom sweet; it is invariably bitter. A measure of truth is included in my speech today, but I offer it as a friend, not as an adversary."

His listeners did not exactly reciprocate his friendship. In fact, many booed when they heard him say that "A decline in courage may be the most striking feature in the West in our day. The Western world has lost its civil courage, both as a whole and separately, in each country, each government, each political party, and, of course, in the United Nations."

Solzhenitsyn's celebrity status was demolished virtually overnight, but his stature as a human being has re-

mained undiminished. *Quid est Harvard?*, one might ask in response to the question posed by Pontius Pilate, *Quid est veritas?*. Solzhenitsyn's wisdom is of perennial significance. As a friend, his audience now reaches far more than those who attended his commencement address nearly 50 years ago. He implores us to honor the truth while advising us that "The simple step of a courageous individual is not to partake in the lie." There is never a time in which this message could be out-of-date.

From Kurelek's Passion of Christ

Chagal's Judgement of Solomon

THE DEMOTION OF TRUTH

I recall listening to a lecture given by a university president. It was clear to me that he was more interested in impressing his listeners with his virtue than enlightening them about his subject, which was the War Between the States. When he had presented his thesis to his mentor, he was told that there are many theories about the Civil War, and it may be that they are all wrong. The president rejoiced in this notion because of its spacious liberality. We can all be researchers without suffering the embarrassment of being more wrong than anyone else.

I thought, in my apparent naiveté, that the Civil War actually took place and that the primary interest of a good researcher lay in discovering the truth of what happened. The truth of the matter, however, seemed to evaporate, yielding to the politically correct notion that we can all be tolerant of each other because nobody is right anyway. The truth is elusive. What is important is liberality, tolerance, and a pluralism of ideas. A university president, I thought, should be made of sterner stuff.

My president would not have been as confident as he was if it were not for the fact that he knew that liberalism was in the air. He was not going to boast that his thesis was any better than anyone else's. He was not going to impose his views on anyone. Nonetheless, he did make a concerted effort to convince the members of his audience of his liberality. I left the lecture hall disgruntled. Truth had been demoted; self-aggrandizement had been promoted.

There is a Latin adage about which most people are familiar: *De gustibus non disputandum est* (Concerning matters of taste, there is no dispute). The corollary adage, about which relatively few are familiar, is: *De veritate disputandum est* (Concerning matters of truth, there must be dispute). Truth is real. Its discovery confers broad benefits, including freeing us from the darkness of ignorance. We should not be complacent about our ignorance. We should dare to make the personal and collective journey toward truth. We are derelict if we do not, being content with but the illusion of liberality.

Pride is the most deadly of the Seven Deadly Sins. It is also the easiest to conceal from oneself. It manifests itself chiefly in three ways: 1) **presumption**, by which we attempt to do things beyond our strength; 2) **ambition**, by which we have an inordinate love of honors; 3) **vanity**, by which we crave the esteem of others. Vanity, in turn, is divided into three vices: boasting, ostentation, and hypocrisy. The person who says, "I may be a lot of things, but I am not a hypocrite," is really boasting, and therefore guilty of pride. The person who declines mentioning that he discovered any aspect of truth may believe himself to be humble, but is really craving the approval of others. Sundry vices ensnare us in the net of pride in so many subtle ways.

Superbia

On the other hand, we need not be boastful if we state something that we know to be true. We know that truth is not of our own making. Its apprehension should stir in us a sense of gratitude, as well as humility. "It is truth, not ignorance," as Jacques Maritain has stated, "which makes us humble, and gives us the sense of what remains unknown in our very knowledge." Moreover, in sharing the truth with others, we are not seeking their praise, but attempting to enlighten their minds. It sometimes requires courage to tell the truth. It never requires courage to hide from it.

There are some Catholic apologists who believe that they would frighten students away if they presented them with the undiluted truth of what the Church teaches. But the essential attractiveness of the Church lies precisely in its truth which has, as Saint John Paul II avers, a certain luminescence or "splendor".

C. S. Lewis was an immensely successful apologist for Christianity without having to dilute it. The British philosopher and self-publicist, C. E. M. Joad read C. S. Lewis. Although Joad was, at the time, an atheist, he praised Lewis, stating that "Mr. Lewis possesses the rare gift of making righteousness readable." Joad, influenced by what he referred to as the "network of minds energising each other," published *The Recovery of Belief* in which he stated his reasons for accepting the Christian faith.

Bishop Fulton Sheen's success in bringing people into the Church is legendary. In no way, did he adulterate the truth to make it appear more palatable. It is the truth, not its shadow, which makes us free. By contrast, the skepticism announced by Pontius Pilate—"What is truth"—does not epitomize the man of tolerance, but one who betrays truth.

Ah! An honest man at last!

ESCAPE FROM CYNICISM

Cynicism results when a person believes that he has conquered hope. Since it is a conquest of sorts, though surely a negative and counterproductive one, it can endow the cynic with a certain amount of pride. In a similar way, a younger brother can take pride in knocking over the tower of blocks that his older sibling constructed. In this case it is pride that goes after a fall. So, too, the cynic believes he has achieved something when he imagines that he has caused either philosophy or theology to topple over. In his own strange way, he finds nihilism, the defeat of hope, to be amusing as the following anecdote suggests.

A philosopher and a theologian were engaged in a disputation. The theologian used the old quip about a philosopher resembling a blind man, in a dark room, looking for a black cat – which wasn't there. "That may be," said the philosopher, "but a theologian would have found it." It is presumed that the philosopher is in search for something that is not there, while the theologian boasts that he has found it.

Its cynicism notwithstanding, this is, in its own way, a good joke. It takes down both the philosopher and the theologian, while making us smile at their alleged pretensions. Here, pride also goes before a fall. But as an afterthought, there is really nothing funny about cynicism. The cynic, as someone has said, is a person who, when he smells flowers, looks around for a coffin.

Diogenes the Cynic, as an historical figure, well personifies cynicism. He became notorious for carrying a lamp in the daytime, claiming to be looking for an honest man. He criticized and embarrassed Plato, disputed his interpretation of Socrates and sabotaged his lectures. He exulted in tearing down anything that was alleged to be noble or important. He was truly an anti-philosopher as well as an anti-theologian. He was the master of the "put-down".

While it is common to poke fun at anything that is pretentious, that demeaning word does not apply to everything that is said to be noble and important. Philosophers were once called "wise men". Pythagoras, took a more modest view of his profession, observing that in the strictest sense, wisdom belongs to God alone. Thus, he coined the term philosophy, meaning "love of wisdom". There is considerable wisdom in his modesty since, at best, we can attain wisdom only in a limited way. The philosopher, as Jacques Maritain has said, is merely "a beggar at wisdom's door".

Yet, wisdom is worth seeking. As St. Thomas Aquinas has remarked, "Of all human pursuits, the pursuit of wisdom is the most perfect, the most sublime, the most profitable, and the most delightful." We often appreciate wisdom in times when we are foolish. Poor Othello, who loved "not wisely, but too well," realized his mistake, but only when it was too late. "Life's tragedy," wrote Benjamin Franklin, "is that we get old too soon and wise too late."

The recognition of foolishness presupposes the existence of wisdom. If foolishness has entered the back door, it is because we have ignored wisdom ringing at the front door. Wisdom is not entirely elusive or incomprehensible. It lies in the proper ordering of things. God comes first, neighbor second, the self comes third. We should think before we speak, look before we leap, and evaluate before we decide. Impetuosity, rashness, thoughtlessness, and carelessness are enemies of wisdom. Cynicism is the philosophy of regret, the painful consequence of choosing things out of order. Therefore, as St. Augustine states, "Patience is the companion of wisdom."

Our ability to recognize the reality of wisdom is evidenced by the immense satisfaction the "Serenity Prayer," attributed to Reinhold Niebuhr, brought to a countless number of people, including members of the armed forces and those dealing with alcoholism and other personal problems: "God grant me the serenity to accept the things I cannot change, the courage to change the things I can, and the wisdom to know the difference." Wisdom here is recognized as the key that gives order to our lives, so that we can do what we can do and not worry about doing the things that we cannot do. The mind has an important role in discovering wisdom. "Cynicism," as Norman Cousins maintains, "is intellectual treason."

The eye is made to see color, the ear is designed to hear sounds, and the lungs are fashioned to breathe in oxygen. So too, the intellect was made to know truth. And truth is a critical stepping stone in the pursuit of wisdom. Again, to quote Aquinas: "The human intellect is measured by things so that man's thought is called true not on its own account but by virtue of its conformity with things."

Philosophy is the love of wisdom and is a great aid in opening the door to theology. It is, as its etymology indicates, an act of love. Therefore, philosophy begins with love. But it also requires humility since it is reality that measures truth, and not the ego. Thus, love and humility, together with patience form a buttress against the invasion of cynicism. Cynicism is neither original nor natural. It is the unhappy consequence of a life lived without wisdom. No child was ever born a cynic. We become cynics by default, as the result of not living a life of virtue and, as a consequence avoiding wisdom, the crown of all virtues.

Seat of Wisdom

THE CASE AGAINST THE PREPOSTEROUS

It would seem unnecessary to build a case against the preposterous. It would seem like arguing against things that are self-evidently foolish, moronic, or idiotic. Yet, there is a certain proclivity alive in society for doing things that are preposterous, a phenomenon that warrants both attention and correction.

This problem came to my attention many years ago when I was teaching a philosophy course to undergraduates. I knew that many of them were in love with what I call "incomplete ideas". Such students championed freedom, but not responsibility, justice, but not truth, and sex without the complications of personal attachment and pregnancy. My challenge was to wean them of their affection for singularity, that is, the mistake of isolating a single idea from its proper matrix and according it supremacy.

I began the course by using three philosophers as excellent examples of thinkers who were skilled at putting several ideas together to form a unified whole. In other words, three philosophers whose thinking was systematic. First, representing antiquity, I chose Plato. Next, as a representative of the Middle Ages, I selected Saint Thomas Aquinas. My third philosopher, exemplifying systematic thought in the modern era, was Mortimer Adler. All of these philosophers, though different in certain ways, understood two important aspects of philosophical thinking: 1) that no idea stands alone, independent of other ideas; 2) that ideas must be placed in the right order and not thrown together willy-nilly.

It was both disappointing as well as astonishing to me that several students could not count to two! As an old cigarette commercial stated, "I'd rather fight than switch". These students held tenaciously to their preferred notion of philosophy, one in which a single, isolated idea (like "choice") was self-justifying. At that point I realized that a case was needed to expose the utter foolishness and unacceptability of the single idea masquerading as a unified philosophy. This is the case against the preposterous.

The study of Latin is often very helpful toward the understanding of words. The word "preposterous" is derived from two Latin words: *"pre,"* meaning "before," and *"posterius,"* meaning "after". Bringing these two words together tells us that to put something "before" which really should come "after" is foolish and unrealistic. It is preposterous, therefore, to try to put one's shoes on before putting on one's socks, or trying to dive into the water before learning how to swim, or trying to erect a third floor without putting in a second floor. The examples are numberless.

It is true that the meaning of "preposterous" has been stretched to include the outrageous and the outlandish. But I wanted to show my students how that word was helpful and appropriate as an argument against the unrealistic assumption that people are free either to choose their own order or to reject the notion of order entirely.

Ecology, which all my students want to protect, involves a great deal of balanced order. We disrupt this order at our peril. Morality is ecological in the sense that one thing follows another according to a predetermined plan. I did not need to convince any of my students of the nature and value of ecology. Morality was an entirely different matter.

Consider the notion of "justice". Everyone is in favor of "justice," especially "social justice". Nonetheless, justice does not stand alone. It is built on truth, just as the second floor is built on the first floor. It is simply preposterous to deny this order. In order to render justice, a judge must discover the truth of what took place. Did the suspect or did he not commit the crime? Justice follows truth. That is the natural order of things. If we put justice ahead of truth, we find that in our preposterous way of thinking, we have completely lost sight of justice. If we put man first and God second, we soon lose sight of God. Similarly, if we put ourselves first and the Church second, we find that we no longer have any need for the Church. In order to preserve things, we must know where they are, which is to say, how they follow or precede other things. A melody can never be preposterous because it consists of the right notes in the right order.

The case against the preposterous is also the case for the proper place and order of things. The formula for JOY, as some clever individual has pointed out, is "Jesus" first, "others" second, and "yourself" third. Former football great Gayle Sayers had the same idea when he titled his autobiography, *I Am Third*.

When sex is isolated from love, commitment, and marriage it becomes difficult to grasp the value of this triad. In the natural order of things, one thing prepares for the reception of what follows. Love prepares the way for marriage, marriage prepares the way for children, and children prepare the way for grandchildren.

That which is preposterous is indeed outrageous and outlandish, but precisely because it inverts the order of reality. Plato, Aquinas, and Adler all agreed that one thing follows another naturally, and not arbitrarily. The natural law is the basis for morality. When people try to suspend morality in space, without any foundation for it, they discover that they have completely lost the very meaning of morality.

The case against the preposterous is needed largely because of its importance. Abortion should not follow conception, divorce should not come after marriage, and despair should not be the consequence of old age. I continue to maintain that, despite the normal frustrations of the educator, teaching should result in learning. The student who thinks he already knows what he has not learned offers us a prime example of the preposterous.

THE DIFFICULTY WITH DIVERSITY

friend and I were enjoying a recreational break by shooting baskets. The fact that we were not keeping score allowed us to engage in a friendly conversation. My friend decided to pick my allegedly philosophical brain and asked me a question that he had trouble answering. He explained that a "diversity expert" had lectured him and all his co-workers that they must all embrace diversity. My friend was uncomfortable about this, but could not put his finger on exactly why he felt this way. This sweet sounding word to our cultured conditioned ears, unfortunately, has become an axiom, and therefore something that cannot be questioned.

Let us question it, nonetheless. I tossed up another shot while it occurred to me that the interchange of ideas might be my favorite sport. Knowing that my friend trusted me offered hope that my response would be helpful. When we clarify our feelings we are able to live with them more comfortably and are better equipped to share them with others. How does one begin to deal with an issue—such as diversity—that has been sufficiently complex and controversial to baffle some of American history's most eloquent debaters? What I write below, I am obliged to say, is not exactly a summary of what I said to my friend, but an extension.

The first thing to understand is that diversity is not a moral principle. It merely describes and array of things that happen to be different. This array may be composed of compatible or incompatible elements. Embracing diversity is not necessarily any better than embracing homogeneity. "Diversity" is descriptive, not prescriptive. It is ironic that in today's world we shun complementarity and champion diversity.

Fine art has been traditionally defined as "diversity within unity". This is a good and helpful definition. Without unity, diversity is chaos, like pearls that have been released from their string. On the other hand, unity with-

29

out diversity is inert, lifeless, uninteresting. Art imitates life in the sense that we are constantly searching for an over-arching purpose that gives meaning to the various episodes of our existence. If diversity is to have any moral significance, it must be wed to unity. To put it simply, the notion of diversity all by itself is incomplete. Diversity in itself is ambiguous and can have opposite interpretations.

Senator John C. Calhoun (1782-1850) believed strongly in diversity, but what he meant by this was the acceptance of slavery and free men as equally constitutive elements. He demanded that the South be recognized for its unique differences, especially its "inequality of condition" that accepted slavery as a fact of life. He rejected the principle expressed in the Declaration of Independence that all men are created equal, stating that it was "contrary to human observation".

Calhoun was hardly alone in acceptance of slavery within the umbrella of diversity. Stephen Douglas, in his debates with Lincoln, denied that a "house divided" cannot stand. He accused Lincoln of being irresponsible for believing that America cannot endure as half-slave and half-free. In rejecting any synthesizing principle, such as the equality of all human beings, he stated that "our government was formed on the principle of diversity . . . and not that of uniformity." He rejected the notion that different people could be held to a single standard of truth or morality, commenting that "We must take them as we find them, leaving the people free to do as they please, to have slavery or not, as they choose." Douglas was also a staunch advocate of being 'pro-choice'.

Lincoln, however, saw the Declaration of Independence as an "immortal

emblem," one that could endure unchanged throughout time. His Gettysburg Address was a rededication to the proposition that "all men are created equal" and the principle of "liberty for all". Lincoln understood that the diverse groups that make up America could be united on a philosophical basis rather than one that was founded on something that was political and, therefore, contingent. Lincoln understood that diversity alone is an incomplete concept. America was founded on the principle that diversity must be organized within unity.

At the present moment, the debate continues. Political correctness, however, has tilted the issue in the direction of diversity alone. Very recently (November, 2016), 60 students and an activist with a bullhorn at Providence College demanded the firing of a prominent faculty member for nothing more than his criticism of the diversity ideology. The victim in this case, is Dr. Anthony Esolen, an orthodox Catholic and author of 16 books and another due for publication next year entitled, *Out of the Ashes: Rebuilding American Culture*. Among his many other accomplishments is his translation of Dante's *Divine Comedy* into English.

It would be an understatement of considerable magnitude to say that political correctness is not a suitable substitute for philosophical thinking, or that the whole is greater than the part. In his fine book, *On Hallowed Ground* (Yale University Press, 2000), the distinguished historian John Patrick Diggins makes the following comment: "Never before in American history has there been such confusion about the meaning of America and the identity of the American people. Never before have Americans been so deprived of the backward glance of historical understanding unsullied by the idiocy of political correctness."

Diversity is an appealing word because it conjures up notions of universal brotherhood and world peace. But it appeals to dreamers who may, in fact, be intolerant toward those who prefer a more complete proposition. Diversity, lest it disintegrate into chaos and confusion, must be understood within the context of an agreeable unity. This is the vision to which Lincoln was dedicated. It is a vision of which we are presently losing sight.

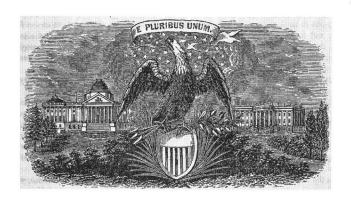

RETREATING FROM REALITY

In his *Way to Wisdom*, the distinguished German philosopher, Karl Jaspers, expands upon his observation that the innate disposition to philosophize is evident in human beings at a very early age. This natural gift of reacting spontaneously to the spontaneity of life, however, is often lost as the years advance. Then, as Jaspers laments, "we seem to enter into a prison of conventions and opinions, concealments and unquestioned acceptance, and there we lose the candour of childhood."

Yet, not everyone, to be sure, loses this "candour of childhood". For whatever reason—a strong character, supportive friends, encouraging teachers, or an insuppressible gift for philosophy—some people remain faithful to that natural disposition all their lives. Nonetheless, the desire to conform, to be in step with the times is very powerful. The natural wisdom of the child often evaporates as a person enters the world to seek his fortune and gain respectability. The siren song of success can seduce a person into bartering his innate sense of philosophy for ideas that are not true, although disarmingly fashionable.

A child knows without having to be schooled that his parents express their love for him in the form of loving acts. The joy the child feels when he opens his Christmas presents is a simple enough example. His gratitude is formed by the happy conjunction of love and deed. There is a natural continuity between a loving conviction and a loving expression. Love is a dynamic impulse that seeks to express itself in appropriate ways. Love is not something that is bottled up in a person for fear that its expression might constitute a wrongful imposition. This is a simple and natural enough point for a child to understand. But with regard to some adults, who see the emperor as regally attired, it is a different matter.

Philosophical errors die hard, if they die at all. 1973 is the infamous year of *Roe v. Wade*. In that same year, Canadian politicians were at work devising a rhetorical strategy designed to mystify opponents into accepting abortion. A clear and concise example of this strategy appears in a 1973 letter written by Justice Minister John Turner to a prominent attorney by the name of Ian Hunter. The letter begins as follows: "One must try to separate one's own private moral convictions from one's sense of duty as a legislator in a pluralistic society to advance the public good." Hunter records his response for posterity several years later in a 1985 issue of *The Idler*: "Of all the vacuous, muddle-headed notions of contemporary politics, this is the most pernicious." Turner had obviously under-rated Hunter's intelligence. Not everyone would be mystified by this nonsense.

"The precise opposite is the truth," as Hunter went on to explain. It is fidelity to one's moral convictions, not their abandonment that is the *sine qua non* in advancing the public good. Does it make the slightest bit of sense for a legislator to say, "I am personally opposed to domestic violence, but I would not try to impose my view on others?" The underlying tacit message is, "Aren't I wonderfully tolerant, broadminded and accepting?"

When a politician is campaigning for office, it is essential, if he has any hope of being elected, to convince people that he plans to carry out his duties. Voters want to be confident they are electing a person who will put his convictions into practice. They do not want to elect anyone who cuts himself off from the public and keeps all his moral convictions locked up in himself. This is an attitude that should disqualify anyone from running for office. The politician or legislator who does not know the difference between ministering to people and imposing alien values is not fit for office. If he thinks that he is an imposer, then he is really an imposter. If one is convinced that justice is a worthy value, then he must do what he can to have it flower.

The reference to a "pluralistic society" is also specious. No matter how pluralistic a society is, it is nonetheless a society and must abide by such universal prohibitions such as murder, larceny, arson, fraud, rape, theft, and other objective disvalues that threaten the good of the people. Abortion is not a trivial issue and most certainly not private. The slaughter of tens of thousands of unborn babies each year in Canada, together with the adverse effects it has on women, marriage, and the family is demonstrably public and not private.

Once a person "separates" his "private moral convictions" from his "duty as a legislator," what is there left for him to do except to do nothing? He has morally eviscerated himself! He is really good for nothing except pulling the wool over the eyes of his voters. We should expect more from our politicians. But we should also expect more from the people. We should expect neither to retreat from reality and find comfort in ignorance.

The errors of 1973 stream into the present and maintain their mystifying power over people. Is it possible to resuscitate reason? At the same time, we witness the shameless attempts to impose the homosexual agenda on people. To minister is essentially different than to impose. A justice minister should not be fearful of ministering or confuse it with imposing.

"Heaven lies about us in our infancy," wrote William Wordsworth, but "Shades of the prison-house begin to close upon the growing boy." How do we avoid entering the "prison-house"? Reason alone is not enough to keep people reasonable. We also need courage and a caring community. "Genius is the re-discovery of childhood," remarked Baudelaire. Perhaps, and more to the point, moral candour is the re-discovery of the innocence of childhood.

Candy Floss Clouds by Kurelek

Plato's allegory of the cave

Parable of the wise and foolish virgins

WE ARE ALL EQUAL IN THE DARK

Being in the dark is not a good place to be. The fact that it makes us all equal offers no consolation. We need light in order to know where we are and how to go about our business. Plato's famous cave dwellers lived in the dark, and since they never experienced the light, were not open to it. Educators would try to vain to liberate them from their predicament. The denizens of darkness, however, preferred to live among shadows and noise. They were all equal, but equally deprived.

Abraham Lincoln was often pestered by advisors who offered him their unilluminated opinions. On one occasion, in the interest of shedding light on the situation, he told the tale of a backwoods traveler who was lost at night in a violent storm. Thunder roared about him. One loud clap, which seemed to shake the earth beneath him, brought the harried traveler to his knees. From this salutary position, he prayed: "O Lord, if it is all the same to you, give us a little more light and a little less noise."

Light is liberating; darkness is not. A liberal education, therefore, provides us with the illumination we need to free us from the bondage of ignorance. But if people have only opinions and no knowledge, such liberation is not possible. It is a grave error to try to educate while at the same time holding tenaciously to the mistaken notion that all opinions are equal. Knowledge is more valuable than mere opinion because it is firmly connected with reality.

At this point we may distinguish between a liberal education and liberalism. In his *Biglietto Speech* when he was raised to the Cardinalate, Jon Henry Newman offered a clear explanation of why he strongly opposed the latter: "Liberalism in religion is the doctrine that there is no positive truth in religion, but that one creed is as good as another, and this is the teaching which is gaining substance and force daily. It is inconsistent with any recognition of any religion, as true. It teaches that all are to be tolerated, for all are matters of opinion."

Newman saw liberalism "as opening the door to evils which it did not itself either anticipate or comprehend." He was both right and far ahead of his times. Could he have possibly envisioned abortion on demand, legalized physician-assisted suicide, and same-sex marriage? A liberal education employs reason in order to acquire a more reliable hold on things. It provides greater freedom *through* reason. Liberalism, on the other hand, is deceptively expansive and progressive because it separates itself *from* reason. Reason is a guide that leads us from opinion to knowledge. It is irrational in the most literal sense of the term to disregard reason in the interest of maintaining a useless equality. Without reason, we do not know how to care for each other.

In his *Confessions*, St. Augustine makes a careful examination of the human condition. "It would be good if men would meditate upon three things to be found in themselves," he writes. "The three things of which I speak are existence, knowledge, will. For I am, and I know, and I will." But if all we have are opinions and no knowledge, we remain in the dark about how we are to utilize our will and stymie our identity at the starting gate. Liberalism is not an education, but a deconstruction of one's personhood. Liberalism is easier than a liberal education. There will always be a group of people who prefer one thing to the other simply because it demands less effort. And so we have fast food restaurants, instant coffee, *French without Pain*, *Shakespeare for Dummies*, and morality without principles. But the value of a liberal education is measured precisely by the amount of work that is required. To remain ignorant costs nothing. But it leaves us groping in the dark.

Mortimer Adler may not have been America's most profound philosopher, but he surely was her most encyclopedic. His passion for the Great Books Program was inspired by his zeal for a truly liberal education. One

must expend energy in order to profit from a liberal education. "The discipline they accomplish," writes Adler, frees us from the vagaries of unfounded opinion and the strictures of local prejudice." By "liberalism," he referred to the view which "confuses authority with tyranny and discipline with regimentation. It exists wherever men think everything is just a matter of opinion. That is a suicidal doctrine."

Christmas is about many things, not the least of which is the importance of light. The December 25th date is grafted on the pagan Festival of Light. Concerning the birth of Christ, Isaiah prophesied that "The people who walked in darkness have seen a great light" (*Is.* 9:2). John the evangelist proclaimed that He is the "True Light coming into the world. The Light shines in the darkness and the darkness cannot overcome it." (*John* 1:5). Christmas lights remind us of the Light that Christ brings into a dark world. They represent the light we need in order to gain a better understanding of each other in this darkened world and the truth we need in order to understand better the greatness of God. Christmas arrives so that we can all be equally bathed in the Liberating Light.

Kurelek's Northern Nativity

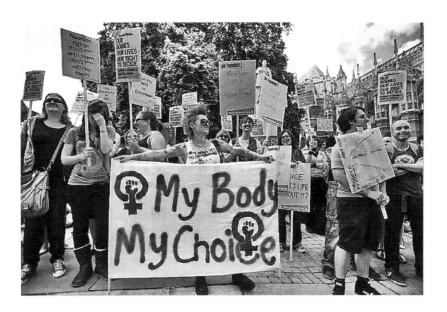

WHO ARE THE BARBARIANS?

The word 'barbarian' originated in ancient Greece. The barbarian (*bàrbaros*) was someone who spoke in a non-Greek language and, therefore, was unintelligible to the Greek ear. The term was specifically directed to Persians, Egyptians, Medes and Phoenicians. It was as though these so-called barbarians were simply uttering "bar-bar-bar". Consequently, the barbarians were incoherent "babblers". Late in the Roman Empire, the term applied to those who lacked Greek or Roman traditions, specifically to Goths, Huns, Vandals, and Saxons.

We have now come to think of barbarians as uncivilized, uncouth, and lacking appreciation for anything outside of their own insular frame of reference. Ironically, according to the modern usage of the term, the real barbarian was the ancient Greek or Roman since they shut themselves off from a broader awareness of things. The modern barbarian is one who regards anything outside of his own frame of reference as incoherent and consequently worthless. He is like the British soldiers during the India rebellion who defaced the Taj Mahal, or Oliver Cromwell going on a rampage, destroying numerous Catholic churches.

Here we may ask the question, "Who is the barbarian? Does the word apply to the Catholic whose doctrine is regarded by many as unintelligible, or to those who do not make the effort to understand the richness of Catholic teaching? The word Catholic, meaning "universal," would suggest that the true Catholic is interested in a wide variety of things. By the same token, the pro-life person, often denigrated as extremely narrow, is interested in defending the life of all human beings.

Alasdair MacIntyre, in his book, *After Virtue*, contends that we are now in the same situation as the ancient Greeks and Romans. With regard to moral discourse, the new barbarians are those who neither speak nor understand the language of the moral tradition that has shaped the relatively humanitarian world we call Western civilization. They regard arguments put forward to defend traditional marriage, the dignity of life, the natural law, and even God's existence as unintelligible. The late Rev. Richard John Neuhaus has added the statement that "Once anyone steps outside this [Western] tradition, then that person is considered a barbarian". C. S. Lewis offered an antidote to the cultural blindness that forms the mind of the barbarian when he advised people "to keep the clean sea breeze of the centuries blowing through our minds . . . by reading good books".

Hilaire Belloc (1870-1953), fittingly known as "Old Thunder," dedicated a chapter called "The Barbarians" in his 1912 book, *This and That and the Other*. He speaks about how we sit by and watch the barbarian and find his antics amusing. To our discredit, we tolerate that which we should oppose. "We are tickled by his irreverence," he writes, "his comic inversion of our old certitudes and our fixed creeds refreshes us: we laugh. But as we laugh we are watched by large and awful faces from beyond: and on these faces there is no smile."

In reading Belloc the spectacle of marches that promote the homosexual life-style come to mind. Their participants live off the capital derived from the very tradition they denounce. But they have no real contribution to make for a replacement. They are a spectacle cut off from both the past and the future. They demand attention but have nothing positive to offer.

Belloc, however, is more concerned about the factors that create a place for the barbarians. He recognizes that society is an organism and as such, it must be able to reject elements that are inimical to it. Therefore, he writes, "Whoever would restore any society which menaces to fall, must busy himself about the inward nature of that society much more than about its external dangers or the merely mechanical and numerical factors or peril to be discovered within it."

Applying Belloc's thinking to the present day world, a weakened society that cannot protect itself against harmful alien elements is like an organism with AIDS whose immune system is too enfeebled to reject harmful substances that attack it. The society that goes out of its way to invite harmful elements into its system is like a society afflicted with AIDS. Belloc's comments, though penned in 1912, are valid for all times.

In returning to the question, "Who are the barbarians?" the answer devolves upon those who have cut themselves off from tradition and regard its contribution to religion, education, and morality as unintelligible. By contrast, the educated person, for whom Plato, Aristotle, Aquinas, Milton, Shakespeare, Bach, Beethoven, Newton, and Einstein are always relevant, is open to the great lessons of history. He is the person who does not allow himself to be limited by either time or space. Nor is his philosophy of life circumscribed by a slogan.

Hence, the person who ignores what science has to say about the nature of the unborn child and rationalizes his position solely on the basis of "choice," would belong to the class of barbarians. Likewise, the reduction of marriage to sex, the dismissal of the natural law, and the disregard for the dignity of life is tantamount to a preference for the barbarian's narrow habitat.

Because society functions as an organism, it must be nourished by what is healthy and it must safeguard itself against what is harmful. There is no middle ground. Human existence is inevitably a relentless moral drama. In his book, *Christian Reflections*, C. S. Lewis put this point in a theological context when he said the following: "There is no neutral ground in the universe: every square inch, every split second, is claimed by God and counterclaimed by Satan."

Civilization, it may be said, is a race between education and barbarism. José Ortega y Gasset alluded to the barbarian assault on modern civilization in his book, *The Revolt of the Masses* (1931), when he referred to "the sovereignty of the unqualified". We need a less affirmative attitude toward the barbarian than tolerance. At the moment we seem to be giving him supremacy.

The Rock by Kurelek

INCURSIONS AND DEMOLITIONS

A friend told me a joke recently that is a better example of theological wisdom than knee-slapping humor: Colonel Sanders bribes the Pope to modify the Lord's Prayer so that it reads, "Give us this day our daily chicken." The Pope agrees, once the bribe is too high for him to resist. At this point the joke is based on the ludicrous incursion of commerce into religion. But there is more. As a consequence of capitulating to Colonel Sanders, the Vatican loses its Wonder Bread account. The Our Father was not, in its original form, a religious prayer at all, but something that was subsidized by a bread company. The initial incursion was only a cover-up for a demolition. Religion had no autonomy. It belonged, heart and soul, to commerce right from the beginning.

The more serious message the joke conveys is that a series of incursions into religion can prepare the way for its demolition. Today, it is politics, more than commerce that is eating away at the integrity of religion, especially that of Catholicism. Former vice presidential candidate Tim Kaine's view that one day the Church will accept abortion is an instance of an incursion that implies a demolition. If the commandment, "Thou Shall Not Kill," and the Church's 2,000 years of clear, consistent and forceful teaching against abortion is wrong, then there is no reason to think that there is anything left in the Church that can resist further incursions.

In discussing the progress of Roman Catholicism in Volume II of his classic work, *Democracy in America*, Alexis de Tocqueville made the following observation which, as things have turned out, had the quality of a prophecy: "One of the most ordinary weaknesses of the human intellect is to seek to reconcile contrary principles and to purchase peace at the expense of logic. There have ever been and will ever be men who, after having submitted some portion of their religious belief to the principle of authority, will seek to exempt several other parts of their faith from it to keep their minds floating at random between liberty and obedience."

De Tocqueville was anticipating the emergence of the cafeteria Catholic who picks and chooses what he wants and leaves the rest on the table. Such a Catholic (and they are numerous) justifies his contradictory stance by claiming that he is "liberal". He does not identify himself with the "doublethink" that George Orwell describes in his novel, *1984*. Typically, he might be obedient to the Church's teaching on social justice while dissenting from Her teaching on abortion. In order to do this, however, he must not allow himself to realize that in approving the killing of innocent unborn children, he is violating the canons of social justice. Killing the unborn is not consistent with social justice since the unborn have a right to continue living.

This cafeteria approach to Catholicism is usually the result of a political incursion. It offers an easy way in which a person can claim to be a Catholic and at the same time find peace among his secular associates. It is not the logical result of a careful understanding of Christianity. It is unimaginable that Christ, who was conceived in the womb, would countenance the killing of unborn children. For de Tocqueville, the prevalence of combining the un-combinable flows from a common intellectual weakness in which logic is scrapped for a certain peace of mind. People do not like to be called "old-fashioned," "religious zealots," "fundamentalists," or even "conservative". Being "liberal" is the popular trend though its magnetic north is the demolition of religion. And this is why Hillary Clinton wants a new religion for America. But what she wants would not emerge from the ashes of an out-of-date Christianity, but, tragically, would be the ashes.

The cafeteria Catholic places himself on shaky ground. When he rejects the integrity of his religion and tries to live a double life, he also rejects logic. For logic demands consistency. As a result, his involvement in secular affairs and his religion are both weakened. But the peace he seeks by compromising his religion cannot be a lasting one. Human beings cannot live a contradictory life and remain in harmony with themselves for very long.

The Catholic historian James Hitchcock has observed the movement from incursion to demolition in Protestant churches. Accordingly, he states that "in each generation, more and more such surrenders [to political pressures] are demanded, until there is finally nothing left, and surrender itself becomes the chief expectation which liberals must meet." Robert H. Bork, in *Slouching Towards Gomorrah: Modern Liberalism and American Decline* made the politically incorrect, though valid assertion that "The president of Notre Dame would much prefer the approvals of the presidents of Harvard and Yale to that of the pope." The temptation to compromise one's faith in adjusting to the demands of the secular world can be very strong even for presidents of Catholic Universities.

De Tocqueville expressed his warning to Catholics in the year 1840. Catholics must meet the challenge, perhaps more than ever before, of living in the world without compromising their faith. In the finally analysis, compromised faith inevitably leads to compromised effectiveness in all social affairs. The wings of the Holy Spirit do not ride on the winds of the Zeitgeist.

Notre Dame president Fr. John Jenkins greets U.S. president Barach Obama

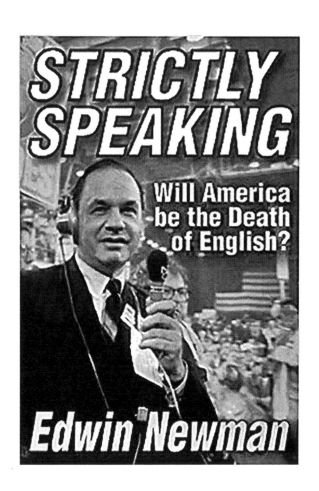

STRICTLY SPEAKING

*S**trictly Speaking* is the title of Edwin Newman's defense of the English language against various assaults coming from politicians, journalists, and other linguistic vandals. *Will America Be the Death of English* is the subtitle. "The outlook is dire; it is a later point in time than you think," according to the former NBC house grammarian. But that was 1974 and his fears have not exactly materialized. We now face a far more pernicious language problem: the pervasive use of perfectly good English words that convey the wrong meaning. I describe, very briefly, ten instances that illustrate this problem, one that threatens both communication and the kind of idealism that is necessary to sustain a civilization.

1) **Authority:** It is commonplace for people to reject authority because they misunderstand the meaning of the word. Authority does not necessarily mean giving orders, but offering reasons. This same fear is commonly directed against parents, teachers, the police and the military. Fear of authority, then, is tantamount to a rejection of reason. The absence of reason, however, invites chaos.

2) **Freedom:** It is not true that freedom is enlarged to the extent that it is emancipated from reason. Freedom is not absolute. Nor is it a terminal value. We are free in the most meaningful sense of the term *through* reason, not *from* reason. Reason grounds us in realism. We are not free because we can fly, but because our feet are on the ground.

3) **Love:** The most commonplace distortion of the meaning of love is to equate it with approval. This is a stagnant notion of love. But love is transformative because it wills the good of the other. Love, therefore, is not the mindless acceptance of whatever the other person does, but a practical concern that is directed to the other's good.

4) **Education:** It is an error of the highest magnitude to believe that education is imposing views on others. One cannot impose a view on another even if he tried. Rather, education is *imparting* worthwhile ideas. It is more like ministering to students' needs to know things that will ben-

efit them, as sunlight ministers to plants. The word "education" refers to drawing out something that is already there, helping students to become more aware of what is inside them. It is not a form of seduction.

5) **Order:** We need order to regulate our lives properly. But that does not mean that our lives should be regimented. We need the proper ordering of the events in our lives so that we can achieve wholeness. The human organism is magnificently ordered so that health is achieved and maintained. Order, in this positive sense, is far from being a form of arbitrary regimentation. It is a form of artistry that brings the parts into unity. Wisdom depends on the proper ordering of our life's actions.

6) **Virtue:** Many pundits have asserted that virtue is its own punishment because it is a weakness that stifles freedom. The opposite, however, is the case. Genuine virtue is a strength that helps a person do the right thing in the midst of temptations to do the opposite. Virtue is rooted in love and directs people to the good. Without virtue, a person wallows in dissipation.

7) **Judgment:** "Do not judge" has become a tiresome cliché. As a consequence, people retreat into the twilight zone of moral inertia. We cannot get through the day without making innumerable judgments. We can neither escape judging or judgment. Judgment need not be avoided for fear of being presumptuous. We need sound judgment in order to distinguish right from wrong. Being able to judge is a human faculty without which we cannot behave in a human way.

8) **Peace:** Though peace is universally desirable, it remains elusive. It is not the absence of conflict but is based on the presence of order. In fact, it is the serenity that we experience when our lives are proceeding according to their proper order. If we want peace, we must put our lives in order. Merely avoiding conflict leaves us with a void that is restive and not tranquil. Peace is not a direct object of choice; it is the consequence of a life characterized by moral rectitude.

9) **Knowledge:** Both the cynic and the pessimist agree that knowledge is nothing more than opinion, that truth is subjective and undiscoverable. Their position, however, is self-contradictory since they believe that their view is the true one. Knowledge is important and should be sought after because it helps us to distinguish between fact and fiction, reason and superstition. Without knowledge that leads to truth, we are left in the dark, hopelessly involved in unresolvable arguments about which no opinion is better than others.

10) **Religion:** For many people, religion is restrictive since they believe that it imposes a dogma on people. Therefore, it is seen as contrary to freedom. The truth of the matter is that religion is a revelation, the illumination of truths that most people would not come to realize on their own. Far from being restrictive, religion is actually liberating. It frees us from superstition and the errors that are the inevitable consequences of pride. Religion lifts us out of ourselves without abandoning us.

We need authority, freedom, love, education, order, virtue, judgment, peace, knowledge, and religion. Without these values, chaos reigns and civilization is just a pipe dream. Yet these values will remain elusive as long as we misunderstand their meanings and choose to view them in their distorted forms. These values represent ideals that are worth the effort it requires to make them a real part of our daily life. They challenge us and reward us. But their realization will not come about unless we are willing to pay the price. Strictly speaking, rectitude and education are better than lassitude and dissipation.

Viking raid on Lindisfarne Monastery

THREE
SLIPPERY WHEN WET

Why I Am Pro-Life
And Not Politically Correct

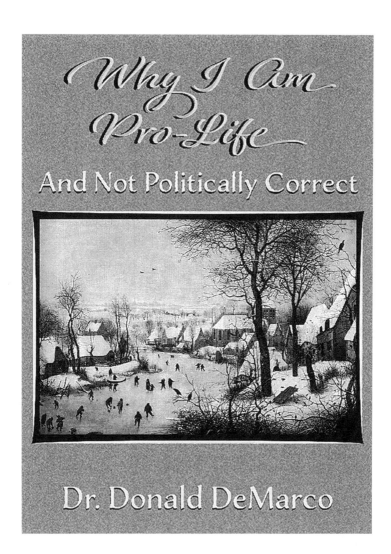

Dr. Donald DeMarco

MADNESS IN THE WORKPLACE

Vatican II *(Lumen gentium* 41*)* reminds us that work provides a road to holiness, because it offers opportunities for: a) self-improvement; b) helping our fellow citizens; c) improving society in general; d) imitating Christ in active charity. On the other hand, as Saint John Paul II states in his *Agenda for the Third Millennium*, "What suffering, what hardship and misery unemployment causes?"

Most unfortunately, however, the Christian notion of the dignity and importance of work is currently being displaced by "political correctness". The distinguished cultural historian, Jacques Barzun, in his compendious work, *From Dawn to Decadence* (2000), makes the blistering comment that "In the United States at the present time the workings of 'political correctness' in universities and the speech police that punishes persons and corporations for words on certain topics quaintly called 'sensitive' are manifestations of the permanent spirit of inquisition." Violations of political correctness are not as harsh as those of the infamous Spanish Inquisition, but often lead to opprobrium, loss of employment and virtual exclusion from one's profession. Nonetheless, as Barzun maintains, the spirit of the inquisition is very much alive today. Barzun's point does not set well with liberals who believe that they have carved out a path that is diametrically opposed to the intolerance and punitive mindset associated with the old inquisition.

Political correctness has made an effective transition from universities to the mainstream workplace. We read in the daily press of individuals losing their jobs because they defended traditional marriage, held to the notion that there are two sexes, opposed homosexual acts on moral grounds, and argued in favor of separate rest rooms for men and women. Barzun contends that university professors "injected 'political correctness' into the academy and made themselves ridiculous by the antics it entailed." Nonetheless, society in general saw merit in the ridiculous and deemed it worthy of imitation.

ESPN is a well-known acronym which, supposedly, stands for Entertainment and Sports Programing Network. Having adopted political correctness, however, it is, these days, looking more like Executives Sub-serving Political Nonsense. Consider the case of legendary pitcher Curt Schilling. The burly right-hander holds the record for the best winning percentage in post season play with 11 wins and only 2 losses. His charitable organization, "Curt's pitch for ALS" supports care for sufferers of amyotrophic lateral sclerosis. When he led the Boston Red Sox to their 2004 World Championship season, after an operation on his ankle, he wrote K ALS on his shoe (short for "strikeout ALS"), knowing that the cameras would give his cause invaluable attention. His weekly radio show raised $100,000 a year for his cause. While he was employed by ESPN, however, he made an unforgiveable mistake and was fired. He offered the politically incorrect opinion that the men's room is for men and the women's room is for women. The network executives' statement read: "ESPN is an inclusive company. Curt Schilling has been advised that his conduct was unacceptable and his employment with ESPN has been terminated."

In his defense, Schilling could have said, "If ESPN is so 'inclusive,' why is it that I am not included?" Does "inclusive" really mean "exclusive"? What, then, would "exclusive" mean? Under the canopy of political correctness, both thought and language are also victims. As Barzun remarked, the language of university professors became "the pretentious garbed in the unintelligible." On the other hand, incomparably more outrageous ESPN activities are simply swept under the rug. James Andrew Miller and Tom Shales have produced a 700+ page book, appropriately titled, *Those Guys Have All the Fun*, which is an embarrassment to the network giant. Their research exposes the huge sex and drug culture that goes on behind ESPN's closed doors. Moreover, 2015 data released by Ashley Madison, a company that arranges adulterous affairs ("Life is Short, Have an Affair," is its well-advertised slogan), indicated that more than 100 members of the ESPN workforce, including influential executives, had signed up for its service. One ESPN producer is reported to have paid more than $2,000 to Ashley Madison. In this macabre sense, ESPN proves itself to be truly "inclusive".

The decline of Christian morality is closely tied to the rise of the bogus morality of political correctness. The BBC has dropped the use of BC (Before Christ) and AD (*Anno Domini*), replacing them with "Before Common Era" and "Common Era". A school is Seattle, WA renamed Easter eggs "spring spheres" so as not to offend anyone who does not believe in Easter. Similarly, in many places, Christmas trees are now known as "holiday trees". A United Kingdom advertisement for a "hard-working" and "reliable" person was rejected because it could offend people who are unreliable and lazy. At the same time, it is deemed unacceptable and inappropriate to refer to anyone as "unreliable" and "lazy". Nonetheless, as the unreliable and the lazy are coddled, the meticulous and the industrious are criticized. It is a topsy-turvy world!

Political correctness has clashed with the Christian notion of work, so beautifully outlined in the documents of Vatican II. How can one survive these days in the workplace? The slightest slip, innocent as it may be under normal standards, can lead to chastisement, sensitivity training, or dismissal. Such an atmosphere is not conducive to happy and productive workers. It may be a sign of progress that most work environments are now smoke free. But it is a clear sign of regress that they, so often, welcome the madness of political nonsense and are poised to punish those who are not in lockstep with their arbitrary demands.

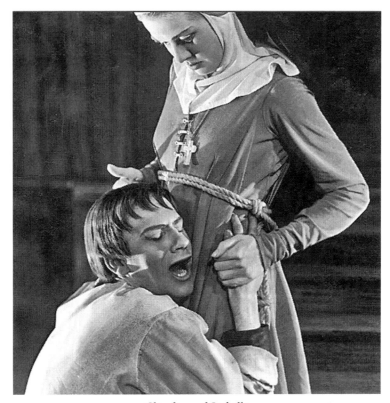
Claudio and Isabella

CAN VICE BE A VIRTUE?

In Shakespeare's *Measure for Measure,* **Lord Angelo**, the temporary leader of Vienna, is committed to ridding the city of its brothels and unlawful sexual activity. He arrests Claudio for impregnating Juliet out of wedlock. He believes that sentencing Claudio to death would serve as a strong example to other Viennese citizens.

Angelo, who, is not a model of chastity, himself, offers to spare Claudio's life if his sister, Isabella, will sleep with him. When Isabella, who is a novice with a cloistered order of nuns, discusses the matter with her brother, she is horrified to discover what a despicable rake he has become as a result of his sexual misadventures. "Death is a fearful thing," says Claudio, who has little regard for his sister's chastity. "And shamed life a hateful," replies Isabella. Claudio becomes more earnest in his plea: "Sweet sister, let me live; what sin you do to save a brother's life, nature dispenses with the deed so far that it becomes a virtue."

He sorely underestimates Isabella's moral sense, thinking that she can be duped into thinking that a vice can be a virtue. It is a line that immediately backfires. Her response could not be more emphatic: "O you beast! O faithless coward! O dishonest wretch! Wilt thou be made a man out of my vice? Is't not a kind of incest, to take life from thine own sister's shame?"

Claudio's excessive preoccupation with sex has poisoned his soul. Isabella wants to have nothing more to do with him, realizing that for Claudio, fornication was not a lapse but a life-style. "Thy sin's not accidental but a trade. Mercy to thee would prove itself a bawd: 'Tis best thou diest quickly." Claudio's misadventures with women means that he was merely using them for his own pleasure. This notion of using women carried over to his own sister, attempting to have someone else use her in a disgraceful manner for his own benefit. Elsewhere, In *Hamlet,* Shakespeare states:

"When the blood burns, how prodigal the soul lends the tongue vows." Lust can blind. It can also deceive. Poor Claudio! his lust had taken possession of him. He could no longer see straight.

Love, as opposed to lust, promotes the good of the other. Using another for one's own enjoyment clearly does not exemplify love. Chastity is the virtue that brings the sexual appetite into harmony with reason. What the distinguished Thomistic philosopher Josef Pieper has said about chastity could have been directed specifically to Claudio: "Unchaste abandon and the self-surrender of the soul to the world of sensuality paralyzes the primordial powers of the moral person: the ability to perceive in silence the call of reality and to make, in the retreat of this silence, the decision appropriate to the concrete situation of concrete action."

Josef Pieper

Chastity needs reason in order to be realistic. Chastity, like all other virtues, are expressions of love. It is reason that ensures that, in a given set of circumstances, chastity honors the person who is loved. A man cannot say, "I love you" to a woman and then expose her to an unwanted pregnancy, rejection, and disgrace. That is no way to treat a lady.

A vice is a vice; a virtue is a virtue. Reason helps us to keep them straight. Nonetheless, when the blood burns, men will continue to profess their love while intending to exercise their lust. Shakespeare, in telling the story of Claudio and Isabella, is on the side of virtue, portraying the ugliness of sin and the attractiveness of virtue. It is a story from which we can all benefit.

HIGHER EDUCATION

Many pro-life advocates believed that the answer to the abortion problem lay in education. Science supports the claim that human life begins at conception. Psychology reports that induced abortion has adverse effects on a high percentage of women. Sociology informs us that abortion has a negative impact on marriage and the family. Scripture command us not to kill. And so on. Unfortunately, education in moral matters has gone underground. Political correctness has not only invaded the groves of academe, but has captured it.

At the same time, political correctness has maintained a veneer of respectability. It is designed to avoid offending anyone while creating the impression that by offering information on both sides of the abortion issue, to take one important example, fairness will prevail. Thus, it is typical of schools of higher education to offer text books that represent both sides of any issue and leave the resolution of the topic to the student. In this way, no one is offended and the student's freedom of choice is fully respected. What is lost in this arrangement, however, is education.

A typical example of this phenomenon is found in a college text prepared by Jacques Thiroux (*Ethics: Theory and Practice*). In offering a justification for abortion, the author states that "women, like men, should have absolute rights over their own bodies." It is simply assumed that men have long enjoyed such rights. Tacitly swept under the rug are a myriad of incontestable realities beginning with mortality and defectibility, and passing through impotence, incontinence, insomnia, and indigestion. Given the power of Kryptonite, not even the fictional Superman has absolute control of his body. It is as if the author began by using some being mightier than Superman as a standard by which he would argue for abortion. This is hardly education.

Blissfully ignoring the fact that he has started on the wrong foot, the author argues that women, in the interest of equality, should also have such rights. He is, of course, pandering to a brace of politically correct notions involving feminism and equality. But his notion of both women and equality are Procrustean. He also adds the myth of progress for good measure. He writes: "In the past, women, because of an 'accident of nature' -- the fact that they are the ones who get pregnant -- have not shared in these equal rights, but now that birth control is possible, they can." At this point, a logically minded reader would protest: "Maybe it is an 'accident of nature' that men do not have the possibility of procreating." Another might say, "Maybe it is an accident of nature that we have legs." At any rate, it dishonors women to assume that their distinctive—some would say 'God-given'-- power to procreate is downgrade to an 'accident'.

What Thiroux does is his "argument" for abortion is to whittle down the nature of the woman so that she looks equal to a man while assuming that men have an absolute right over their body which, of course, they do not have. And this becomes, what he calls, "the central argument" for justifying abortion! He is counting on the word 'equality' to blind his readers to the obvious fact that he is comparing two fictions to each other.

Thiroux erroneously identifies contraception with 'birth control'. He then adds to this mistake by identifying birth control with abortion, thus displaying his ignorance of the meaning of all three terms ("abortion [is] just another method of birth control"). The truth is, nonetheless, that contraception aims at preventing a pregnancy; abortion ends a pregnancy that has already begun. "Birth control" is a misnomer that has little to do with either birth or control. As G.K. Chesterton once quipped, "They insist on talking about Birth Control when they mean less birth and no control."

Not finished with his parade of errors, the author then boldly asserts that "any conceptus is a part of a woman's body until it is born." Here, he is exposing his ignorance of science. Giulio Cesare Aranzi (*Arantius*; 1530-1589) showed that the blood systems of the fetus and the mother are neither continuous nor contiguous with each other. Thiroux is five centuries behind the times. Moreover, the fetus has its own DNA, has received half of its genes from a male and has its own sex type, which may also be male.

The author, in being eager not to offend the naïve reader, manages to infuriate those who are intelligent. He wants to be neutral by presenting both sides as if they had equal merit (if he is really pledged to equality, he should look at the gross inequality in credibility he has established between the two sides he represents). Political correctness attempts to conceal deeper truths in order to maintain a superficial ideology.

A colleague of mine, teaching at a state university, tried as hard as he could, to present both sides of the abortion controversy as fairly as possible. Nonetheless, he was criticized by some of his students for making the pro-life side appear to be more attractive. Such students, sworn to the myth of neutrality as they were, could not believe that the pro-life side was inherently more attractive. Neutrality is not a virtue, nor is it an end in itself. A baseball umpire should be neutral about which team wins, but he cannot be neutral about balls and strike, and whether a player is safe or out.

Moral neutrality can be dispelled through knowledge. In a world of pure neutrality, no one would ever have a conviction strong enough to act on. "I used to be indecisive, but now I'm not so sure," does not illustrate progress. The whole point of education is to move from neutrality, indecision, ignorance, apathy, or indifference to knowledge, conviction, wisdom and action. The text book approach, by trying to make both sides seem equal is designed to prevent education from taking place. It stops the process of enlightenment at the starting gate. It fails to teach while seducing students into believing that they are being educated.

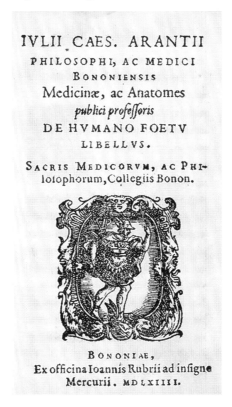

IS DIVERSITY A VIRTUE?

A Harvard undergraduate who, when his confreres were asked to list what they believed to be their virtues, wrote: "I am diverse". In the kingdom of political correctness, there is no word that is more highly revered than diversity. Yet many are blinded by the glow of this fine sounding term. Of course, one person alone cannot be "diverse," but more significantly, a virtue must be acquired. Furthermore, one cannot practice diversity and real virtues must be put into practice. Virtue is not possessed by everyone simply because they call themselves "diverse".

This gross misunderstanding of both diversity and virtue, comical as it may be, opens the door to a problem that is not only pervasive in the contemporary world, but has been a long standing problem in American history. Diversity without unity is chaos; unity without diversity is a stifling uniformity. How is it possible in the political realm, as opposed to the world of art, to harmonize diversity and unity? Sensible educators have posed the searing question whether the minds of college students should be developed or converted politically.

When Abraham Lincoln famously stated that a house divided against itself cannot stand, he was underscoring the importance of unity and harmony. He was fearful that conflicting factions could be ruinous for the country. At the same time, he recognized that America needed a common purpose, which is to say that it must also be "united". Stephen Douglas took strong exception to Lincoln's position. He argued vehemently that the country could endure being half-slave and half-free. "Our government," he declared, "was formed on the principle of diversity . . . and not that of uniformity." Douglas was both a champion of diversity as well as a proponent of choice. He argued that the architects of the Constitution "knew that the laws and regulations which would suit the granite hills of New Hampshire would be unsuitable to the rice plantations of South Carolina." He denied that there could be any moral foundation for judging either the morality of slavery or the moral object of personal freedom.

Thus, diversity, for Douglas, is a non-negotiable fact, while choice is severed from justice.

Douglas (as well many others at the time) believed in "diversity" and "choice". But his brand of diversity and choice would be completely unacceptable in today's climate. Nonetheless, his philosophy is identical with that of contemporary diversitarians and pro-choice advocates. The very same philosophy undergirds two utterly antagonistic results. Here is clear evidence that we are not clear-headed when it comes to philosophizing. We draw from the same well both what we believe to be poison as well as what we believe to be nourishment. We naively believe that the Islamic terrorist and the Quaker can lie down together in peace.

Lincoln was a true philosopher. Even in a democracy, he stated, "people do not have a right to do wrong". In so saying, he appealed to the Declaration of Independence which proclaimed that all people are created equal and endowed with certain inalienable rights. Thus he could remark, concerning a black female slave: "In her natural right to eat the bread she earns with her own hands without asking leave of someone else, she is my equal and the equal of all others." Lincoln's concept of diversity extended to all people and was not limited to special groups, as it continues to be the case in today's world.

St. Thomas Aquinas and St. Augustine warned against what they called "counterfeit virtues". According to the Angelic Doctor, a virtue must be directed toward a good. But if it is directed toward what is only "an apparent good, it is not a true virtue that is ordered to such a good, but a counterfeit virtue." For Augustine, "the prudence of the miser, whereby he devises various roads to gain, is no virtue; nor the miser's justice, whereby he scorns the property of another through fear of punishment." Both Aquinas and Augustine teach that all virtues must be based on love, which is to say that love is the form of all virtues.

Dorothy Sayers, noted essayist and mystery writer, has devised her own set of counterfeit virtues which she calls the Seven Deadly Virtues. They are: Respectability, Childishness, Mental Timidity, Dullness, Sentimentality, Censoriousness, and Depression of Spirits. Her seven stand as a parody of the seven foundational virtues consisting of the four cardinal virtues (justice, fortitude, temperance, and prudence) and the three theological virtues of faith, hope, and charity. Sayers is keenly aware of the fact that where true virtue is lacking, counterfeit virtues swoop in to take their place.

It should be clear enough that "diversity" is not a virtue. But false virtues camouflaged in the same language as authentic virtues may be more difficult to expose. Compassion is popularly regarded as a virtue. When it is used, however, to rationalize killing the innocent, it is clearly a bogus virtue. We can say the same of the courage of the bank robber, the mercy of the doctor who euthanizes his patients, and the loyalty of the criminal whose allegiance is only to the syndicate.

There is an additional problem with diversity. It is a fine and noble thing to acknowledge the humanity of various groups of human beings and to refrain from offending them in any way. This alleged virtue, however, extends only to carefully selected groups such as feminists, homosexuals, racial minorities, and transgendered persons. Excluded from the list are pro-life advocates, Evangelical Christians and orthodox Catholics. Such diversity, of course, is a hoax. Nonetheless, being spellbound by the word "diversity," diversitarians are blinded by their own presumption of being virtuous.

We are in love with the idea of love. Yet we are reluctant to accept the difficulties and disciplines that real love requires. Therefore, we accept a bogus love that expresses itself in counterfeit virtues to be more attractive. Real love—genuine concern for the good of others—is independent of politics. It is primarily personal and self-giving. And it is only through love that true virtues can be expressed. Therefore, virtue is a delivery system that brings the good of the lover to the needs of the one who is loved.

THE FETUS AND THE FUTURE

The Amazing Criswell introduces *Plan Nine from Outer Space*, widely acclaimed as the worst movie ever made, in a declamatory style designed to terrify members of the audience: "Greetings, my friend. We are all interested in the future, for that is where you and I are going to spend the rest of our lives. And remem-  ber, my friend, future events such as these will affect you in the future." The events to which he refers involves grave robbers from outer space set to destroy planet earth. All of this, he tells us, is "based on sworn testimony". Criswell was better known for his wildly inaccurate predictions (for example, that an Interplanetary Convention would take place on March 10 in Las Vegas sometime during the 1980's featuring representatives from Mars, Venus, Neptune, the United States, and the Moon). He was an appropriate choice, therefore, to set the tone for *Plan Nine*, beseeching God to "help us in the future". His performance may very well have earned him the distinction of being the worst, if not the most unintentionally comical, narrator in the annals of screendom.

Anything that is the very worst in a category, especially where there are numerous candidates, is particularly fascinating. What is the worst song title of all time? A worthy candidate would be *They Needed a Songbird in Heaven, so God Took Caruso Away* (1921). What is the worst movie title of all time? It would be hard to ignore *The Incredible Strange Creatures Who Stopped Living and Became Mixed-Up Zombies* (1964).

What is the worst argument for abortion, one might ask? And indeed there are many candidates. We look to Princeton University's Center for Human Values and philosopher Elizabeth Harman for our answer. In a July 25, 2017 You Tube presentation, she contends that the fetus does not have moral value because, if aborted, it has no future. According to Harman, we have "moral value in virtue of our future". And since the about to be aborted fetus has no future, neither does it have moral value. Therefore, aborting a young fetus is not a moral issue. It is "derivative of its future that it [the fetus] gets to have moral status."

If Liz Harman sounds a little like the Amazing Criswell it is because they both manipulate the future so that it seems to be in the present. Criswell consults the present to assure us that we will have a future. Harman consults the present to determine that the fetus does not have a future. Both Criswell and Harman are predictors, the former promising a future that might be terrifying, the latter predicting that the present fetus will have no future.

Harman's argument requires a distortion of the time line. Let us imagine two separate fetuses of the same age. One will, presumably, be aborted, the other will be born. According to Harman's calculus, the former has no future and consequently no moral value, the latter has both a future and moral value. This cannot be determined empirically, but only hypothetically. If the fetus is aborted, then, retroactively, it did not have moral value in the past. If it is not aborted, retroactively, it did have moral value in the past. The present is incomprehensible, however, since there is no way of predicting accurately whether a fetus will or will not be aborted. Pregnant women have been known to change their minds about abortion one way or the other. We do not look at the fetus living in the present to determine either its nature or its value. We skip over the present and hypothesize about an unpredictable future.

One person, after watching the You Tube, asked, "How is it possible to be so well educated and completely void of critical thinking skills? This is a good question and begs for a good answer?" Another reviewer states: "This is why you should not go to university. You end up heavily in debt, and extremely stupid."

Omitted from Harman's reckoning is the fact that the reason an aborted fetus has no future is precisely because it is aborted. By extension, no person, if killed, has a future. This removes the stigma from all killings. Unwittingly, Harman has found a justification for homicide: well, since we killed this person it did not have a future, and therefore did not have any moral status. Her argument, of course, is circular. Killing is permissible since the deceased had no future. Therefore killing is self-justifying. No wonder another person who watched the You Tube presentation said, "Isn't that how Hitler justified killing Jews by taking away their personhood?" If personhood and moral status is derived from the future (as if anything could be derived from the future) then killing someone, born or unborn, does away with an agent that has no moral status.

Harman commits the fallacy of "begging the question," a distortion of logic in which it assumed that the conclusion can validate the premise. For example: I know that God exists because it says so in the Bible, and I know that the Bible is trustworthy because it was inspired by God. According to Hartman: I know that abortion is moral because the fetus does not have a future, and I know it does not have a future because it will be aborted. Hartman does not prove that abortion is moral, but she does beg that it is. But logic relies on reasoning to a conclusion, not begging for one.

Ms Harman should reflect on the natural sequence of time: past, present, future. The present is derived from the past, not from the future. The future does not yet exist and therefore cannot be the cause of something in the present. The future is derived from the present and the past. The future is unknown. It cannot dictate to us in the present. It cannot determine our moral choices. The future is best understood as what we bring to it out of our past.

FOUR
POOR VISIBILITY

Where Am I? Who Am I? Why Am I?
William Kurelek

THERE ARE NO HUMAN BEINGS

The contention which has been put forth by several writers that there are no human beings will seem rather startling to most people. After all, such claims are made by those whom we usually refer to precisely as human beings. Nonetheless, although most people would agree that there are human beings, the consequences of this strange philosophy are very much with us today and will be difficult to expel without a clear understanding of their roots. The flowers and the trees are eminently visible; it is their roots that remain in hiding.

Jean-Paul Sartre argued, insistently and consistently, that there are no human beings (*"Il n'y a pas de nature humaine"*, as he stated in his major work, *Being and Nothingness*). This total negation of human nature, for Sartre, derives from his radical atheism. If there is no God, he maintained, then there is no one to conceptualize human nature. Therefore, when we are born, we only exist. It is through our life's choices that we obtain an essence, though it has no name and belongs uniquely and exclusively to the individual. Consequently, existence precedes essence.

Sartre accorded absolute value to choice, since it is through choice that we obtain an essence. As a result, we cannot be held responsible for our choices. We do what we do through our freedom in determining who we become, for our bare existence to gain an essence. On this premise, Sartre can write sentences that should shock most people: "The most atrocious situations in war, the worst tortures do not create an inhuman state of affairs; an inhuman situation does not exist." If there is no human nature, there cannot be anything which is inhuman. Absolute freedom prevails.

Sartre is by no means alone in this kind of thinking. Walter Kaufman, a German-American philosopher who taught at Princeton University for more than 30 years (1947-1980), firmly agrees with the fundamental principle of existentialism, laid down by Sartre, that "existence precedes essence." Accordingly, he writes the following: "Thus, there is no human nature, because there is no God to have a conception of it. . . . Man is nothing else but that which he makes of himself. That is the fundamental principle of existentialism. . . . We define man only in relation to his commitments; it is absurd to reproach us for irresponsibility in our choice."

This type of freewheeling moral philosophy that entitles a person to choose anything he wills without reproach or recrimination, is cheerfully accepted by those who advocate abortion on demand, the unqualified right to euthanasia, sex without regulation, and marriage without structure. But its range of enthusiasts is ever-widening. If there is no human nature, how can there be sexual natures? The eradication of human nature leads logically to the eradication of all natures within the individual. Consequently, even one's sex is something to be chosen. Humanity, sexuality, and marriage are all assumed to be nature-less. But a world without natures is a world without guidance.

Existentialism, it should be noted, is not restricted to atheistic thinkers. Soren Kierkeaard, a Christian existentialist, affirms that whoever has no God has no Self, and who has no Self, is in despair. F. H. Heinemann, in his work, *Existentialism and the Modern Predicament*, claims that "A society adopting this attitude [that of Sartre and Kaufman] would be ripe for the rubbish-heap." Dostoevsky stated that "If God did not exist, everything would be permitted." And that "everything" would include war, famine, and pestilence. And let us not forget G. K. Chesterton's bon mot that "if there were no God, there would be no atheists."

We read in Jeremiah 1:5 that "Before I formed you in the womb I knew you; before you were born I set you apart." And in Psalm 139:16: "Your eyes have seen my unformed substance; And in Your book were all written the days that were ordained for me, When as yet there was not one of them." In his encyclical, *Humani Generis*, Pope Pius XII condemned atheistic existentialism because of its irrationalism, subjectivism, pessimism, and because of its degradation of human reason."

God is telling us through Scripture that our essence, that is, our human nature, is something that He has endowed us with. In other words, it is God, not the individual, Who accounts for essence. Existence does not precede essence, it is coterminous with it. Our duty in life, therefore, is not to choose anything we like, since there are no essences and consequently no moral guidelines, but to choose in a way that is consistent with the human nature that God has given us. This makes it possible for people to live together in peace and harmony.

According to William James, a new theory goes through three stages. In the first stage it is attacked as absurd. Next, it is regarded as true, but obvious and insignificant. Finally, it is heralded as so important that even its adversaries claimed that they themselves discovered it. It is hoped that the idea that neither God nor human nature exist will be returned to the first stage and recognized for the absurdity that it is. Meanwhile, many people are searching for a basis of morality that all can share and a way to accept their natures not as some arbitrary thing to be chosen, but as God-given treasures to be honored and cultivated.

PLAN ONE FROM OUTER SPACE

The life of every person is an unfolding story. The plot, however, is not always clear. We plan our lives, but our best laid plans are often turned awry. It has become a cliché that if we want to make God laugh, we tell Him our plans. Our plans are spoiled by the whims of chance or sabotaged by the plans of others. And when out plans fail, we adopt another plan that is subject to the same fate.

God has His own plans for us. It would have been negligent of Him to cast us into the world without providing us with a plan. Although we must keep on planning, we must acknowledge that God's plan has top priority. "Plan One From Outer Space," we might say, is part of God's gift to us. Our plans—from one to nine—are inevitably short-sighted and marked for failure. "There is no road has not a star above it," wrote Ralph Waldo Emerson. When we subordinate our plans to God's, we begin to discern the development of our authentic story. Our road to meaning requires supernatural guidance.

Our plans are linear. They can end. We plan a picnic, but it rains. We plan to get to the theater on time, but get caught in traffic. We plan a delightful vacation, but the weather is persistently inclement. We do not have possession of the Master Plan that coordinates all plans. The linear plan is for one, God's Plan is for everyone.

If rational plans can end in disappointment, they cannot end with pleasant surprises. We cannot plan to be surprised. When C. S. Lewis writes about "being surprised by joy," he is alluding to something that cannot be planned. Joy-filled surprises come from outside of planning. Life would certainly be dreary if there were no surprises. Moments of happiness take us by surprise. They seize us; we do not seize them. In addition, there would be no humor without the element of surprise. "The secret to humor is surprise," said Aristotle. Excessive planning leads to a gloomy and humorless life. We need a higher plan, one that we cannot conceive on our own.

The poet Robert Browning has made the remark that "all human plans and projects come to naught". When one plan is fulfilled another plan takes its place. Graduation from high school gives way to graduation from college, securing a job, buying a house, and so on. One flies to Chicago, then taxis to a hotel, proceeds to the dining room, finds his room, etc. Each plan, when fulfilled, reaches its destination and steps aside for another plan. One's destiny, however, remains unfulfilled. When we plan, we have a series of destinations in mind. God has our destiny in mind, and it is one that can be fulfilled only by adherence to His moral laws. And that destiny is to be fully ourselves, what God intended us to be.

The Swiss psychologist, Carl Jung, in his autobiography, *Memories, Dreams, Reflections*, relates a dramatic instance of a plan gone horribly awry. He describes what happened to a female doctor, a member of society's upper crust, who confessed to him that she had poisoned her best friend in order to marry her friend's husband. She had been confident that her crime would go undetected and that she would not experience any remorse. A series of misfortunes, however, proved her wrong. Her new husband died shortly after her marriage, relatively young, and his daughter from his earlier marriage withdrew from the fold as soon as she could. According to Jung's account, even animals, including her favorite horse and pet dog, turned away from her. She was so struck by the silent verdict of both her friends and her animal companions, that she was plunged into unbearable loneliness. Jung's judgment, which he left for the reader, is harsh, though not unrealistic: "She was a murderess, but on top of that had murdered herself. For one who commits such a crime destroys his soul."

Plans that violate God's Commandments are essentially incompatible with one's destiny. Our plans must be consistent with the moral order. If a person wants to make God weep, one might say, tell Him that by having access to abortion allows a woman to gain control of her destiny. God's Plan is convergent in the sense that it is co-ordinated in order to accommodate the plans of more than one person at the same time. Thus, God has a plan that synchronizes the destinies of husband and wife within the context of marriage, as well as the destinies of a mother and her unborn child. God's Plan harmonizes a multiplicity of individual destinies. Only God could arrange things in such a manner. Our own linear plans belong to the realm of tunnel vision. On our own, we are incurably myopic.

Abby Johnson's exposé, *Unplanned Parenthood* (2010), reveals the severe short sightedness of Planned Parenthood. God's plans for the unborn are thwarted by abortion. He is the Creator; abortion is the de-creator. Abortion contradicts both the destinies of the mother and her unborn child. Planned Parenthood's "plans" are regressive. They cannot be coordinated with a higher destiny. They implode upon themselves. Abby Johnson learned what Planned Parenthood has yet to learn, namely, the supremacy of God's Plan. In her words: "Everything about my journey since running out of the Planned Parenthood clinic into the waiting arms at the Coalition of Life house was unplanned—by me, I mean. I look back in the journey and see God's fingerprints all over it." She goes on to say that the one seed she wants to plant in the hearts of everyone who hears her story it is that "God is worthy of our obedience and trust. When we step out in obedience, God rolls out the red carpet (p. 207)."

Be it done unto me according to thy word.

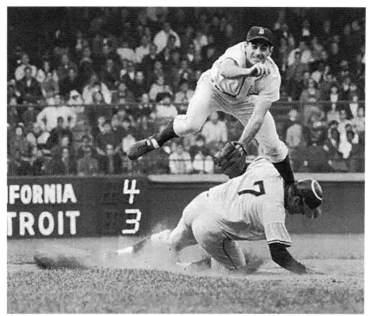

Safe at third

Out at home

SAFE AT THIRD, OUT AT HOME

  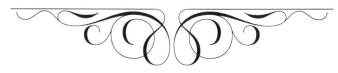

When I was very young, I assumed that I was destined to come into being even if my mother had married someone other than the person who became my father. I knew nothing about genetics. "It doesn't work that way," my biological parents said to me. They left it at that, being reluctant to get into the nitty-gritty of things.

It left me wondering, however, about the improbability of my existence. I was glad that my mom and dad met and married each other. But I was glad for much more than that. Once I learned something about genetics and heredity, this improbability zoomed into the realm of the unbelievable. Of my father's millions of sperm, just the right one had to mingle with just the right one of my mother's hundreds of thousands of eggs, in order for me to exist. The chances of me being me was infinitesimally close to zero. To make the situation even more mind-boggling, the same improbable exchange of gametes had to occur between all my paternal and maternal genealogical ancestors in order for me to exist and possess my unique set of genes. Perhaps God had a guiding hand in all this. What was apparent, however, was the fact that from a statistical point of view, I probably should not be here. My gratitude, therefore, should be commensurate with the unlikelihood of my unique existence.

Looking at things from a cosmic perspective, let us divide my genealogical history into three stages. The first includes the vast amount of time that transpired from my primal parents to the coming into being of my mom and dad. All the right gamete exchanges had to occur into order for my parents to come into being. The second is the fact that of all possible partners, my parents chose each other to marry. The third stage is the moment of conception when the one sperm of my father and the one egg of my mother that were needed to form me united with each other. I must value my existence, since, from the viewpoint of probability, it was so highly unlikely to occur.

Now, looking at things from a perspective that is much easier to imagine, let us relate these three stages to a baseball diamond. Getting to first base took eons. Getting to second base required just a few years. Getting to third base needed only a few days. Now that a person is safe on third, which corresponds to the mother carrying him in her womb, the long history of improbabilities have put him in a position in which home is within relatively easy reach. Here, poised at third, one is very close to the end of a journey that is as long as it is improbable. And yet the last lap, seemingly the shortest and least improbable, is routinely annulled by abortion. It is a crime of cosmic and historical proportions. It closes the drama just before it can reach its triumphant climax.

The saguaro cactus is considered an adult when it has reached 125 years of age. Its average life expectancy is between 150 and 175 years. Given how long it takes to mature, it is highly valued. Saguaro cacti are protected by law. In the year 2007, Gregory McKee and Joseph Tillman were charged, under Arizona's "Lacey Act," with cactus poaching and sentenced to eight months in a federal prison. "This activity will not be taken lightly," stated Dennis K. Burke, U.S. Attorney for the District of Arizona, "Creative landscaping is no excuse to plunder natural treasures from our national parks." Robert Love, the Chief Ranger at Saguaro National Park, made the comment that "Saguaros have become a valuable commodity and are increasingly targeted by thieves and poachers. Sentences like the ones imposed on Tillman and McKee send a strong message to those who plunder our Nation's natural resources."

The longevity of the saguaro cactus is the mere blinking of an eye in comparison to the eons of time required to produce a unique human being. Yet, it is a crime to dig up a cactus and a mere "choice" to exterminate an unborn child.

In 1945, William J. Cameron wrote an inspirational essay entitled, *Don't Die on Third*. It was reprinted by the Ford Motor Company as an instructional guide conveying the message not to give up when one is close to the finish line, or "not to die on third". The concluding paragraph reads as follows: "So, while there's one thing yet to do, and there's always one thing yet to do, or a fraction of time to do it in, Don't die on third. Study conditions, learn all you can, use all you learn, summon your strength and courage, defy luck — and, then, bold player — just by doing this, you have already scored. Something great is strengthened within you." The message was intended to transcend baseball.

How more appropriate is this advice when applied to the woman who is carrying a child — a child of the universe — and contemplating an abortion! Sports, at their very best, can be an inspiration to life. But sports should never be a replacement for it. We often take sports too seriously, and human life not seriously enough. Nonetheless, being safe at third, out at home, is the great tragedy of our time.

THE LIMITS OF EQUALITY

It should be sufficiently evident that not all human beings are equal in every way. Equality is a "Great Idea," as philosopher Mortimer Adler notes, but it does not relate to every aspect of the human being. Nature has placed limits on it that cannot be denied without impunity. Human beings, as the Declaration of Independence states, are created equal. Consequent to this equality is equality under the law and other equalities that pertain to the dignity of man. People are equal in their humanity, but they differ markedly in natural endowment and in personal achievement. To stretch the notion of equality to the extent that it denies these two factors is both unrealistic as well as unjust. And there is, as history shows, a steep price to pay for this denial.

We have observed, in recent memory, a denial of the specific roles of mothers and fathers under the umbrella term, "parenting". Likewise, "husband" and "wife" have lost their distinctiveness, being replaced in many instances by "partner". This is especially the case with regard to same-sex marriages. In Spain "mother" and "father" no longer appear on birth certificates, having been replaced by "Progenitor A" and "Progenitor B". In some cases, ascribing gender to a newborn is deemed politically incorrect.

Recently, the Metropolitan Transit Authority has outlawed the use of "ladies" and "gentlemen" by employees of the New York train system. These traditional terms are now replaced by "passengers". The process of stretching equality to conceal real differences does not make people more equal but denies them their specific identity. To refer to a woman as a "lady" honors her femininity and reminds both men and women how she should be treated. The same can be said for the term "gentleman". It reminds men how they should conduct themselves, especially with regard to the opposite sex. The words "ladies" and "gentlemen" are not opposed to equality. Rather, they recognize and honor specific identities. If we think that we are all the same in every way, we lose sight of who we are and how we should treat each other.

It has been truly said that if we do not understand the mistakes of history, we are condemned to repeat them. Experiments with extreme equality (or egalitarianism), from a historical perspective, have proven to be colossal failures. The French Revolution abolished the terms "*madame*," which literally means, "my lady," and "*monsier*," which literally means "my lord". Men and women became known as "citizens" (*citoyen* for men and *citoyenne* for women). The deposed King Louis XVI became *Citoyen* Louis Capet. In his classic work, Reflections on the Revolution in France (1790), Edmund Burke predicted that the radical egalitarianism in France, reducing all levels of society to a basic equality, would have disastrous results. He correctly predicted that the revolution would not bring about more liberty for the individual but war and dictatorship. It was not until 1815, after the dictatorship of Napoleon Bonaparte, that peace would return to Europe.

Burke penned his celebrated work as an attempt to discourage the start of a similar revolution in England. "Society is a contract between the past,  the present and those yet unborn," he wrote. He saw the revolution in France as disruptive, breaking ties with tradition and losing momentum for future generations. His reasoning is worth noting to dissuade America from embarking on the same destructive path. Burke's writings and speeches earned him celebrity status throughout Europe. He died in the year 1797 when the fate of France and Europe was unsettled. However, he lived long enough to see his predictions come true. During the Reign of Terror, there were 16, 594 official death sentences in France between June 1789 and the end of July of the following year. The guillotine claimed the lives of between 17,000 and 40,000 French citizens.

History reveals a similar trajectory from extreme equality to dictatorship in other countries. In Russia, after the Bolshevik Revolution, leftist revolutionaries adopted the term "Comrade" (*tovarishch* in Russian). In China, the translation of "comrade" was *pinyin*, literally meaning people with the same spirit, goals, and ambition. The Central Committee of the

Communist Party of China issued a directive in October 2016 urging all the 90 million of its party members to continue to use this equivalent of "comrade" in addressing each other.

It is an historic irony that extreme equality has so often produced not a level playing field but a dictatorship. By definition, a dictator is radically unequal in his powers compared with those whom he rules. This irony can be at least partly explained by the fact that extreme equality, being extremely unnatural, can be maintained only by governmental force. In North America today, although there is much grumbling about the campaign to eliminate traditional notions of male and female, mother and father, husband, and wife, and so forth, the czars of political correctness hold great power and influence.

Saint John Paul II composed his *Theology of the Body* to offer the modern world an integrated vision of the human person. This vision includes the significance of the body and how men and women, consistent with Scripture, are simultaneously equal, distinctive, and complementary. It was a monumental accomplishment that required 129 Wednesday audiences over a period of six years, dating from 1979 to 1984. "The human body," he stated, "includes right from the beginning ... the capacity of expressing love, that love in which the person becomes a gift — and by means of this gift — fulfills the meaning of his being and existence."

Extreme egalitarianism disregards the importance of the body, reducing the human being to an abstract generalization. Realistically, however, men are men, and women are woman, wives are wives, and husbands are husbands. A government that does not respect nature will inevitably suffer a revolt from nature. Marriage and the family are founded in nature and not by government fiat. Equality must be limited so that personal identity can be allowed to flourish.

Bosch's Mockery of Christ

Kurelek's Mockery of Christ

FROM DEBATE TO MOCKERY

I have been involved, on several occasions, in public debates on the issue of abortion. Ideally, the debate is a noble endeavor in which two sides, with different views on a subject, put forth their best arguments while respecting their worthy opponents. In my experiences defending life as a debater, the debate has been far short of this ideal. I recall one occasion in which I was expounding on a scientific point I had culled from the writings of Sir William Liley, the Founder of Fetology, when I noticed a peculiar reaction from the audience. I turned around quickly and observed my worthy opponent gesticulating with his hands and making funny faces. He was more interested in mocking his opponent than involving himself in the fine art of debating. In this case reason took a back seat to mockery.

My debating experiences have left me with the conviction that I was never debating with a particular opponent, but against culture in general. This is a losing battle, although it might win a few individuals who have respect for reason, science, and facts. An episode from *Seinfeld*, considered by many as the best TV comedy of all time, illustrates the point. Kramer enlists Poppie's support for the zany idea of a pizzeria in which the customers make their own pizza. Their cooperative venture quickly turns to debating whether customers have the right to choose whatever topics they desire. "On this topic," Poppie insists, "there can be no debate". Presumably, Poppie is pro-choice when it comes to the selection of toppings. The discussion then shifts to when does pizza become a pizza. Is it when you first put your hands into the dough or not until it comes out of the oven? The intended parallels with the origin and development of life are clear: kneading the dough with fertilization, the oven with the uterus, and emerging from the oven with birth. This is all done for laughs. But it is a mockery of the dignity that the formation and development of new life deserves. It is hardly a debate. Pro-life advocates, presumably, are trying to squeeze truth out of a joke.

In Shakespeare's *Othello*, the evil Iago plants seeds of doubt in Othello's mind about his wife's faithfulness. "O, beware, my lord, of jealousy; it is the green-ey'd monster, which doth mock the meat it feeds on." Here, the Bard may be referring to a cat who plays with the mouse before it kills the meat it feeds on. We were all, at one time, fetuses, though not in an oven, but in our mother's womb. Are pro-abortionists mocking their own genealogy when they take abortion so lightly? Are they mocking the very meat they feed on?

We have isolated abortion from life, meaning, and justice, and reduced it to a choice, thereby making a mockery of new human life. Novelist D. H. Lawrence made the same point with regard to isolating love from all transcendent values. "We are bleeding at the roots," he wrote, "because we are cut off from the earth and sun and stars. Love has become a grinning mockery because, poor blossom, we plucked it from its stem on the Tree of Life and expected it to keep on blooming in our civilized vase on the table." For Lawrence, such isolation was a "catastrophe". Love, like life, belongs to a network of supporting and interweaving values.

The typical debate involves two sides: the "pro" and the "con". It should not be taken too seriously. It is merely a microcosm of a much larger debate that is going on throughout history. Mocking is a weak, momentary and ineffectual assault. In the end, truth and justice will prevail. In Galatians 6:7, St. Paul tells us: "Be not deceived; God is not mocked: for whatsoever a man sows, that he shall reap." God's truths will not collapse under the weight of mockery. The correlative point is that those who mock Him should be concerned about where their philosophy is leading them.

We laugh when we see that things are out of joint, contrary to the right order. But when things are in their proper order, we admire them and are glad. Laughter may be the best medicine, but we do not want to be taking medicine all our lives. When we are healed, we can get back to enjoying life more fully. Seinfeld is funny. Nonetheless, the nihilism that undergirds the show has little to contribute to human happiness. One laughs until he cries if he cannot find anything to which he can dedicate his life. In another Seinfeld episode, George Costanza, brooding over the discoloration on his lips and fearing that he will never become a TV celebrity, says, "God will never let me enjoy success." Jerry then asks, "I thought you didn't believe in God," to which George replies, "For the bad things I do". Here is the tragedy of nihilism in a nutshell: in the absence of a God who can give meaning to our lives, we need to invent one to complain against. We cannot be entirely godless; one bad god is better than no god at all.

Seinfeld will not have the last word on the abortion debate, though it does appeal to the group mind that is formed by the Mass Media working in tandem with personal inertia. Friedrich Nietzsche, the founder of modern nihilism, once remarked that man laughs because "he suffers so deeply that he had to invent laughter". He was referring to himself, not to everyone. The best laughter, however, and there are many kinds, comes out of an abundance of spirit. Feast days, birthdays, anniversaries are fine occasions for setting the mood for laughter and gaiety. We should not expect too much from a television comedy.

If debate has degenerated to mockery on the abortion front, there is no need for despair. We may still draw inspiration from a Russian proverb reiterated by Alexander Solzhenitsyn in his 1970 acceptance speech for having won the Nobel Prize for literature: "One word of truth shall outweigh the whole world."

Rouault's Mockery of Christ

FIVE
FOG PATCHES

LEAD US NOT INTO TEMPTATION

"**I can resist anything but temptation**," quipped Oscar Wilde. His remark is really more humorous than cynical. But it does underscore a truth, namely, that there is some measure of difficulty for all of us in resisting temptation. Even the saints had to wrestle with temptation. "I am delighted with the law of God according to the inward man," writes St. Paul, "but I see another law in my members fighting against the law of my mind, and captivating me in the law of sin that is in my members" (*Rom.* 7:15).

Temptation is an ever-present problem. "Opportunity knocks but once", as a pundit once remarked, "But temptation leans on the door bell". In this case, the exaggeration brings the point into high resolution. Temptation is something we need to deal with on an almost constant basis.

In the sixth petition of the Lord's Prayer, we ask God not to lead us into temptation. This is the most baffling of all the seven petitions. Would God lead us into temptation? On the one hand, St. James tells us that "God tempts no man" (*James* 1:13). On the other hand, we read in *Genesis* 22:1 that "God tempted Abraham". What appears to be a contradiction, however, opens the door to a most important and illuminating distinction.

In Fr. Francis J. Remler's insightful book, *How to Resist Temptation*, the author explains that there are two different kinds of temptation. He calls one, "the temptation of probation". By this, he refers to the trials that God sends us that we need in order to grow to spiritual maturity. The probation officer hopes that his ward will prove, over the period of probation, that he is sufficiently trustworthy to be given a wider range of freedom. We need trials and challenges to prove our fidelity to God. These temptations, like those visited upon Job, are purifying. Therefore, God tempted Abraham in this sense.

Fr. Remler identifies the second kind of temptation as "the temptation of solicitation". In this case, the person "solicits" or welcomes temptation. This is the form of temptation that God does not introduce. It is the temptation that we ourselves choose, directly or indirectly. Someone once said that women flee temptation, but men crawl away from it cheerfully hoping that it will overtake them. This would exemplify, with due apologies to all men, the indirect form of temptation.

The distinction that Fr. Remler makes between the two kinds of temptation is most helpful. Nonetheless, in the interest of simplicity, I would like to make a parallel distinction between a "trial" (that God sends us) and a "temptation" (which we invite upon ourselves). Consequently, when we ask God not to lead us into temptation, we are not requesting that He spare us trials, but that when trials arrive, we do not misinterpret them precisely as temptations. In other words, we should regard trials as an opportunity for purification. Job proved to be steadfast and faithful and was justly rewarded. He did not view his trials as temptations to despair. His trials had a positive function, not a negative one. Thus, we should regard our trials in a positive sense and remain firm in our conviction that God will help us to understand them in this way.

In the first volume of his three volume opus, *Jesus of Nazareth*, the then Pope Benedict XVI states that "*The Book of Job* can also help us to understand the distinction between trial and temptation. In order to mature, in order to make real progress on the path leading from a superficial piety into profound oneness with God's will, man needs to be tried." Nevertheless, trials are dangerous. Although they are indispensable as paths which purify the person as well as binding the person closer to God, they do offer him an opportunity to fall. Hence, all the more significant is the petition in which we ask God not to lead us into temptation.

The expression "pride comes before a fall" illustrates the intimate relationship between a temptation and a negative outcome. The proud person is tempted to believe himself to be more important than he really is. He has an unrealistically inflated view of himself. As G. K. Chesterton has described it, "Pride is the falsification of fact by the introduction of self." Being top-heavy with illusory self-importance, the proud man is bound to fall. In this way, as Chesterton goes on to explain, "Satan fell by the force of gravity," whereas "angels can fly because they take themselves lightly". We should not take ourselves too seriously. Again, as St. Paul warns us, "He that thinketh himself to stand, let him take heed lest he fall" (1 *Cor.* 10:12).

Trials are humbling. They teach us that we are not self-sufficient and constantly rely on God's saving grace. They help us to form a stronger relationship with God. "Even saints must be held by the hand of God," writes Fr. Remler. "The moment they let go of it, perhaps thinking they need His help no longer, or the moment He stops holding them up, in punishment for their pride or want of charity, they are bound to fall and sustain serious injuries in doing so."

Cardinal Newman remarked that a thousand difficulties do not make a single doubt. So too, a thousand trials do not make a single temptation. Keeping in mind the distinction between a "trial" and a "temptation" helps us to appreciate the critical importance of relying more on God and less on ourselves. Lead us not into temptation also means, help us to understand the salvific meaning of your trials and give us the grace to accept them in accordance with your Will.

Édouard Goerg, etching for Le Livre de Job

Destiny

CONTROLLING MY DESTINY

"Destiny" is a word that has both profound and mysterious significance. And like kindred words such as love, beauty, goodness, wisdom, and truth, it is often trivialized to fit some mundane purpose. A football team, for example, is said to "be in control of its own destiny" simply because its trip to the playoffs is not dependent on a rival team losing. Yet, that same team is not in control of winning. Nor does it make any sense to say that at the start of the season every team is in control of its destiny. Equally fallacious is the notion that contraception and abortion afford a woman "control over her destiny". We have no control of how words are cheapened or used in a contradictory fashion, but we can do something about restoring important words to their more exalted meaning.

The truth is that "destiny," in its proper sense, is something that no one can ever be in control of. The central paradox of destiny is that it comes to me from the outside, although, in some way, it is present within myself. Destiny, therefore, must be from God. "There is a divinity that shapes our ends," says Hamlet, "Rough-hew them how we will". "That is most certain," replies Horatio" (Act V. Sc. 2).

For Chaucer, "The destiny, minister general, that executeth in the world over-all, the purveyance, that God hath seen before . . . All is thus ruled by the sight above" (*The Knightes Tale*). Destiny involves a mysterious interaction between our freedom and God's superintendence. It is a matter of coordination, not control. It cannot be determined simply by a "Destiny Number," which is calculated by adding the numbers associated with each letter of a person's name.

Destiny involves the God who created us and did not abandon us to chance. It is interesting to note that the word "density" is an anagram for "destiny". This is most fitting since, there is an anthropological basis in us for our destiny. Our destiny is rooted, in part, in our particular makeup. Caruso's destiny was to sing, Rubinstein's to play the piano, Michelangelo's

103

to be a sculptor, Bernadette Soubirous to see the Immaculate Conception, Karol Wojtyla to become Pope John Paul II. A horse cannot sing like a nightingale, nor can a nightingale whinny like a horse. Destiny is neither a matter of chance nor of fate. It is the fulfillment of our faithful relationship with God's Will.

The fact that we have a destiny is a source of great hope and jubilation. It means that we are not abandoned to "the slings and arrows of outrageous fortune". It means four things in particular that add challenge and excitement to our lives:

1) **My destiny is unique.** Because of the particular way in which I was made, given whatever talents and abilities God has given me, my destiny is unlike that of anyone else's destiny. Therefore, I can pursue something which is mine in a most specific way.

2) **My destiny awaits me.** Because God has shaped my destiny, it is something that has pre-existed in God's mind. Thus, my destiny is something real.

3) **My destiny is achievable.** By living in accordance with God's Will, it is possible to achieve my destiny. Therefore, I can live with hope and have faith that my destiny can be realized.

4) **My destiny is worthwhile.** Because God has a hand in my destiny, it must be something that is good and worth whatever sacrifices I must make, and hardship I must endure along the way. I will not succumb to the grim notion that "The paths of glory lead but to the grave."

Our destiny, though it draws us like iron fillings to a magnetic pole, remains elusive. We understand full well what "destination" means. I drive to the airport and complete one destination. This is followed by a series of additional destinations: my flight to New York, my ride to the hotel, taking the elevator to my room, and so on. As I complete one destination another destination immediately takes its place. But, as I go through this process of completing one destination after another, am I any closer to my destiny? Destinations do not deliver one's destiny. Destiny transcends destination. When I am asked "Where are you going?" it is always in terms of reaching another destination. I do not know how to speak of my destiny though I know, deep in my heart, that I have one.

In his book, *The Destiny of Man*, Nikolai Berdyaev discusses destiny as the process of advancing from mere individuality to spiritual personhood. "Individuality is a naturalistic and biological category," he writes, "while personality is a religious and spiritual one." An individual is part of the species, is born and dies. But personality is created by God. "It is God's idea, God's conception, which springs up in eternity." Thus, man's destiny is to achieve spiritual personality: "personality," for Berdyaev, "is a task to be achieved".

A communist government may have a "Plan" for its people. But this plan is not unique to each person and has nothing to do with the dignity of the human person. Destiny, though shrouded in mystery, belongs to each of us as a reality conceived by God that draws us out from the finitude and pre-occupation with the self to a richer realization in spiritual personhood. And as this transformation takes place, we begin to understand both the reality and the rewards of our specific destiny.

Last Judgement by Brueghel

BROTHERHOOD WITHOUT FATHERHOOD

Saint John Paul II made a claim in his international best-selling book, *Crossing the Threshold of Hope*, that may be startling to many, namely, that Original Sin, is, above all, an attempt "to abolish fatherhood". Upon reflection, this statement makes a great deal of sense. After all, Adam and Eve chose to reject God and side with the serpent. This initial act of disobedience, or Original Sin, has cast a shadow that has covered all of human history. For the former Holy Father, the notion that God is not a loving Father, but as a tyrant or oppressor, has led to a rebellion against Him as a slave would rebel against the master who kept him enslaved. Whether God is a loving Father or an oppressor is perhaps the most fundamental of all moral questions.

In addition to the attempt to abolish the Fatherhood of God, is the outright rejection of Him. This rejection has an immediate impact on society in that it also represents the rejection of all forms of fatherhood. Writing for the *American Psychologist*, authors Louise B. Silverstein, and Carl F. Auerbach assert that "the argument that fathers are essential is an attempt to re-instate male dominance by restoring the dominance of the traditional nuclear family with its contrasting masculine and feminine gender roles" (*Deconstructing the Essential Father*, June 1999). A concerted attempt has been underway in the last few decades to "deculture" paternity. Fatherhood is something bad.

The attempt to abolish Fatherhood is by no means restricted to academia. For example, on the cover flap of Philip Pullman best-seller, *The Golden Compass* (which was made into a popular movie), the author offers us a brief description of his theology: "My sympathies definitely lie with the tempter. The idea that sin, the Fall, was a good thing. If it had never happened we would still be puppets in the hands of the Creator." Moreover, as he continues to inform us, "I am all for the death of God." "My books are about killing God." "I am of the Devil's Party and I know it." For Pullman, the principal evil in *The Golden Compass* is called "the Authority".

As a direct consequence of the derogation and dismissal of fatherhood, additional weight has been placed on "brotherhood". The "rainbow coalition" and all groups that profess to be "inclusive" exemplify this transition. Yet, there cannot be any true brotherhood without fatherhood, just as there cannot be offspring without parents.

David Blankenhorn has provided compelling evidence in his critical study, *Fatherless America: Confronting Our Most Urgent Social Problem*, that fatherlessness is the most harmful trend of the current generation: the leading cause of the declining well-being of children; the engine driving our most critical social problems, from crime to adolescent pregnancy to child sexual abuse to domestic violence against women. Such warnings, however, go largely unheeded and are casually dismissed as tradition-bound, or arch-conservative.

As fatherhood diminishes, mother-nature becomes more central. Hence the intense, sometimes extreme, interest in ecology, the environment, and planet earth. The disappearance of the vertical dimension has led to an exaltation of the horizontal. The relationship with God the Father has been replaced by relationships between kindred groups bearing various, often elongated acronyms. Godfried Cardinal Danneels' questions are worth pondering: "This feverish search for all sorts of communities, large and small—could it have anything to do with the obliteration of the Father? Is universal brotherhood possible in the absence of a common Father?" (*Handing on the Faith in an Age of Disbelief*). The key word here, is "feverish". For the Belgian Cardinal, it implies a kind of desperation.

The type of community group to which Archbishop Danneels is referring, tends to be self-justifying. Its members are usually protective of each other and abhor any criticism from the outside. They do not have lofty aspirations but merely ask for acceptance. Such an arrangement is the antithesis of Christian community that does not dissolve its relationship with God the Father. The Gospel tells us, "Be perfect, as your heavenly Father is perfect" (*Mt* 5:48), and "when you have done all that is commanded of you, say, 'We are unworthy servants'" (*Lk* 17:10).

The Father can command, because He is the loving authority who has given us our life. But He can also forgive us our trespasses and restore us to spiritual health. Without the Father, therefore, three important factors are absent: the gift of life, the command to use it well, and the readiness to forgive. A community lacking in these three factors, even if it calls itself a brotherhood or a coalition or an alliance, is, by comparison, impoverished.

John the Evangelist, in his First Letter (*Jn* 2:1-2), speaks to us with great solicitude and warmth: "My little children, I am writing to you so that you may not sin; but if any one does sin, we have an advocate with the Father, Jesus the righteous; and he is the expiation for our sins, and not for ours only but also for the sins of the world". All forgiveness is from the Father, whose concern extends to everyone, everywhere.

Brotherhood needs Fatherhood just as children need parents. The rejection of God the Father will continue to have calamitous results. Brotherhood is of the present. Fatherhood not only unites us with the past and with the future, but with eternity.

A NEW PSEUDO-ARGUMENT FOR ATHEISM

An amateur theologian and an amateur plumber have something in common. They know a few things, but should enlist the services of a professional when their problems are more than they can handle. I have a friend who is a self-styled theologian. He has never had a theological problem with suffering. He contends that suffering can strengthen character, elicit loving care from others and serve a redemptive purpose. Christ is the ultimate role model for all who suffer because he showed how Good Friday can lead to Easter. So far, so good. But my friend feels that he still has a strong argument for atheism. Although he believes that "all this suffering in the world" does not repudiate the existence of God, "all this stupidity in the world" does. After all, sayeth my friend, Christ was not stupid and stupidity never accomplished anything. Furthermore, the amount of stupidity in the world, according to his cal-

culus, is utterly staggering. He was fond of buttressing his argument by quoting his rock icon Frank Zappa who once remarked that "There is more stupidity than hydrogen in the universe, and it has longer shelf life." Case closed!

Socrates encountered a self-styled theologian in Plato's dialogue, *Euthyphro*. After an extended conversation, the Gadfly of Athens could not convince Euthyphro that God is good not because some say He is good, but because He is good in Himself. Euthyphro insisted that something is what it is because he says it is. His view was later reiterated by crooner Dean Martin: "You're nobody 'til somebody loves you." Euthyphro was too involved in himself to take a peek at reality. He was too much caught up in his status as a soothsayer. He was a "know-it-all" who was completely lacking in self-knowledge. Socrates encountered many such individuals who could not see beyond their own noses. Yet, despite these experiences, his belief in God was never shaken.

The Greek word *logos* was adapted by John the Evangelist to describe God as "The Word": "In the beginning was the Word, and the Word was with God and the Word was God" *(John* 1:1). John describes the Incarnation of Christ when he tells us that "The Word was made flesh and made His dwelling among us" *(John* 1:14). The term *logos* (*verbum* in Latin) also means "reason". Christ, therefore, is a model of reason. In imitating Him in this regard, we think and behave in a reasonable way and in so doing, avoid being stupid.

Einstein, who did believe in God, though not exactly the God of Abraham and Isaac, once stated that "the difference between stupidity and genius is that genius has its limits." The great physicist must have been fond of this notion, for he offered it to us in the form of a variation: "Only two things are infinite, the universe and stupidity, and I'm not sure about the former." For the misguided liberal, genius is far too confining. God decreed in *Genesis* that there are two sexes, male and female. Saint John Paul II developed his massive *Theology of the Body* around this point. At an international conference on women, feminists were arguing that there are at least five genders. But this number, in retrospect, was rather tame. A recent New York City ruling states that there are 31. Not to be outdone, "face-book" claims that there are 58. Others, jumping on the band wagon, assert that there are at least 63 genders. Stupidity, as Einstein recognizes, is boundless, and therein, perhaps, lies its appeal. What havoc do we reap, however, if we systematically urge children to believe that they can choose from a catalogue of more than sixty genders for themselves!

If we are less foolish and more reasonable, we become more Godlike. We are, after all, rational creatures. By utilizing reason in our daily life, we express our gratitude to the gift that God gave us. Widespread stupidity is not an argument against the existence of God. It is an indication that we should be more reasonable so that, by being imitators of the Word, it is easier for us to affirm God's existence. Stupidity may be pervasive, but it is not incurable.

Stupidity that is hardened and persistent, nonetheless, is a serious problem. Reverend Martin Luther King, Jr. noted that "Nothing in all the world is more dangerous than sincere ignorance and conscientious stupidity." Scripture warns us that "when your eye is bad, your whole body is filled with darkness. And if the light you think you have is actually darkness, how deep that darkness is! (*Matthew* 6:23). Christ is not only the Word incarnate, but the Light. The presence of stupidity does not mean the absence of God.

Pope Leo XIII clearly recognized the values of both the light of natural reason and the light that is provided on a supernatural level. In his encyclical *Aeterni Patris*, on Christian Philosophy, he offers us the following statement that is a source of clarification as well as encouragement: "For, not in vain did God set the light of reason in the human mind; and so far is the superadded light of faith from extinguishing or lessening the power of the intelligence that it completes it rather, and by adding to its strength renders it capable of greater things."

GRAY MATTER

St. Thomas Aquinas stated in the second chapter of his *Summa Contra Gentiles* that if he were writing for the Jews, he would use the authority of the Old Testament, and if he were writing for Christians, he would use the authority of the New Testament. But since he was writing for the Mohammedans who do not accept the authority of either, he must "have recourse to the natural reason, to which all men are forced to give their assent."

Reason is the common denominator of all human beings. It represents the possibility of turning discord into concord. The rejection of reason is the rejection of something that is essentially human and therefore leads to violence. Turning our attention to the civil strife involving the conflict between black and white that continues to plague America, reason represents the primacy of "gray matter" since that is the color of the brain and is a natural way of reconciling black and white.

Black lives matter, and so, too, white lives matter. All lives matter. But so does gray matter matter. The coolness of reason offers hope for understanding and reconciliation. Reason is in accord with truth and justice. When reason is rejected, so are these indispensable virtues. The universal value of reason should not be contested. Let us all be reasonable.

Certain recent events in the United States involving a disrespect for the flag have led to intense controversy. It is said that an athlete has a right not to honor the flag when the National Anthem is being played at the beginning of a sporting event. There are many rights a person has which are imprudent and counterproductive. The range of rights far exceeds that of the range of good ideas. A person has the right to paint his house bright orange, or wear a five foot hat to work, but these are not good ideas. It seems that many Americans have forgotten the significance of their own flag and why it should not be disrespected.

Francis Scott Key provided an important piece of Americana when he wrote the lyrics to his country's National Anthem, "The Star Spangled Banner". The circumstances that inspired his immortal words constitute a significant and dramatic moment in American history. It was the War of 1812. The British had been bombarding Fort McHenry for 25 hours. Scott Key, a lawyer, was aboard a British ship negotiating a prisoner exchange. He was not allowed to return to shore and had to watch the bombardment 8 miles away. The British finally gave up trying to destroy the fort, allowing the smoke to clear. The lawyer, who was also a poet, strained to see whether the flag could been seen. "By the dawn's early light," he could see those "broad stripes and bright stars". Each of his four stanzas ends with reference to the "star-spangled banner" waving triumphantly, gloriously symbolizing "the land of the free and the home of the brave".

The song gained immense popularity and was played during public events, such as July 4 celebrations. On July 27, 1889, Benjamin Tracy, Secretary of the Navy, signed a general order making *The Star Spangled Banner* the official song to be played at the raising of the flag. It was played during the seventh inning stretch at each of the 1918 World Series games and became a staple preceding innumerable sporting events after that. President Herbert Hoover signed a bill in 1931 officially adopting "The Star Spangled Banner" as the national anthem of the United States of America.

The flag represents an ideal. By disrespecting the flag, one is, at the same time, disrespecting that ideal. One may protest the evil he sees in many ways. As former US Representative Ron Paul has remarked, "Real patriotism is a willingness to challenge the government when it's wrong". But to denigrate the ideal that the flag represents is to attack the very reality that one hopes will remain intact. It is a contradictory strategy. It is like slapping your dad in the face and then asking for a raise in your allowance. It is rejecting the ideals and then demanding their implementation. The ideal is unassailable; it is the deviation from the ideal that should be corrected.

Congressman Joe Barton calls to our attention the fact that "Our flag honors those who have fought to protect it, and is a reminder of the sacrifice of our nation's founders and heroes. As the ultimate icon of America's storied history, the Stars and Stripes represents the very best of this nation." And Ronald Reagan warned that "If we ever forget that we are One Nation Under God, then we will be a nation gone under."

Reason tells us not to bite the hand that feeds us or to kill the goose that lays the golden eggs. In 1861, Oliver Wendell Holmes, Sr. added a fifth stanza to the *Star-Spangled Banner* that includes the following words which are a severe indictment against anyone who fails to respect the flag:

If a foe from within strike a blow at her glory,
Down, down with the traitor that dares to defile
The flag of her stars and the page of her story!

To protest the flag is to make a protest that is so broad that nothing remains to serve as the matrix for improvement. In the absence of the pincushion, the pins have no home. Gray matter indicates that if we want improvements to be made, we ought not to rail against that which stands to receive the improvements. Reason tells us to avoid strategies that are self-destructive and adopt those that preserve the fount while correcting the flow.

The Maze by Kurelek

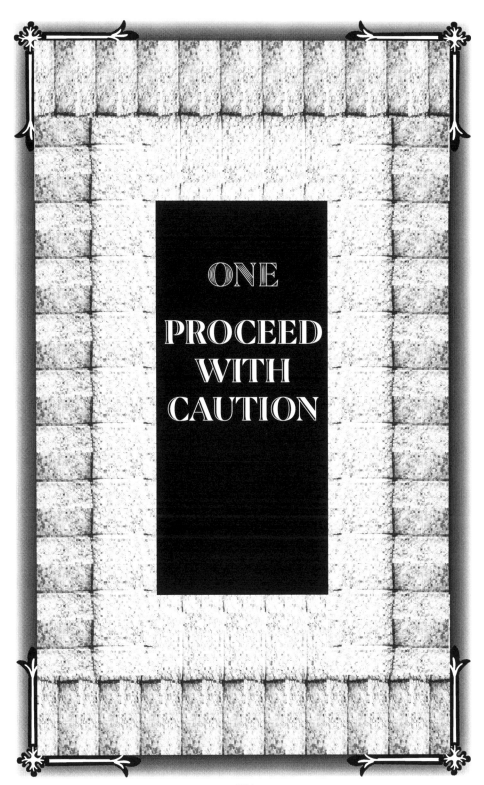

PHILOSOPHY AND THE UNEXAMINED LIFE

The prospect of undergoing a medical examination can be a source of acute anxiety. Who knows what fearful things the doctor might find! Nonetheless, ignorance is not bliss and medicine provides great potential benefits for everyone. We should look upon the medical profession with benevolence, not anxiety.

Socrates was not a medical doctor. He did, however, strongly advocate examinations. "The unexamined life is not worth living," is perhaps his most celebrated phrase as well as his most important directive. Putting one's life on the examination table, however, may be a more fearful thing than submitting to one that is purely physical.

As a philosophy teacher, I assume the role of Socrates. I operate without stethoscope or scalpel. My approach, therefore, seems relatively harmless. I am confined to a world of words, those airy vessels that are intimately bound up with thoughts. I am not like the medical doctor. I do not diagnose, administer anesthesia, operate, or seek to provide a cure. I merely invite my students to undertake their examinations on their own. And yet, I am met with strong opposition.

I recall introducing to my *Philosophy of Discontent* students one Louis Marinoff, who, in the tradition of Socrates, seeks to help his clients examine their own lives and utilize the benefits of philosophical thinking. What a wonderful thing it is to be able to think. What would we be without the power of thought? "Man is but a reed, the weakest thing in nature," Pascal famously stated, "but a thinking reed." "By space," he added, "the universe embraces me and swallows me up like an atom, by thought I embrace the universe."

Thinking can be liberating, enjoyable, beneficial, and uplifting. Dr. Marinoff, a professor of philosophy at the City College of New York, is one of a dozen or so philosophers in the United States who try to help people—one on one—to clarify their thoughts and utilize philosophical thinking with the goal of living a better and happier life. I am helping people "through dialogue," he writes, "to lead a more examined life." He has incorporated his thoughts in *Plato Not Prozac: Applying Philosophy to Everyday Problems* (2000). And yet, like the Gadfly of Athens and many other philosophers before him, he, too, is persecuted. The president of the American Psychiatric Association, for example, has expressed his outrage over what he believes to be Marinoff's invasion into medicine. "This guy," he claims, "is practicing medicine without a license and is approaching a major medical violation."

In my naiveté, I assumed that my students, especially since they were studying philosophy, would be supportive of Marinoff. To my surprise, they were not. Most of them sided with the medical hegemony. I suddenly became a student in my own classroom. Why is it, I thought to myself, that they would support the powerful medical establishment against an isolated philosopher who merely wants to help people by engaging them in dialogue? The answer seems apparent. We live in a "Therapeutic Society". According to Philip Rieff, the author of *The Triumph of the Therapeutic*, "Religious man was born to be saved; psychological man is born to be pleased. The difference was established long ago, when 'I believe,' the cry of the ascetic, lost precedence to 'one feels,' the caveat of the therapeutic." The therapeutic society is a culture which systematically encourages people to expect from life a sense of total well being achieved at little cost, and based on a complete rejection of any moral demands that society places on the individual self. Thinking can be hard. Moreover, it takes time and therefore does not fit into the expectations of a push button or quick fix culture.

Although the sales of the antidepressant, Prozac, has deceased in recent years, the name retains its metaphorical significance as characterizing a society that places more faith in pills than in philosophy. In addition to the title of Marinoff's book, we find *Prozac Nation* by Elizabeth Wurtzel; *Bet-*

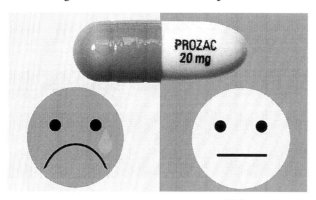

ter Living: In Pursuit of Happiness from Plato to Prozac by Mark Kingwell; *Potatoes Not Prozac* by Kathleen Des Maisons *et al.*; and *Prozac: Panacea or Pandora?*

While anti-depressants have their legitimate role to play within medicine, one wonders to what extent they are crowding out what clear philosophical thinking can do for people whose real needs are nothing more than an honest examination of their own lives. Socrates is still relevant, though like the Maytag repairman of TV commercial fame, rarely called upon. People persist in believing that they get only what they pay for. The Socratic Method comes without cost.

Malcolm Muggeridge once envisioned a modern and trendy St. Paul who was looking for advice in how to promote the Gospel more effectively from a public relations expert. "Well, you've got to have some sort of symbol," the expert would say. "Well, I have one," St. Paul would reply. "I've got the Cross." Then, according to Muggeridge, "the public relations expert would have laughed his head off. You can't have anything like that . . . It's absolutely mad."

"Men have the power of thinking that they may avoid sin," wrote St. John Chrysostom. What can be more discomforting to people than to examine their lives and recognize their need for confession? Yet, confession is reconciliation and a return to a fuller and happier life. I owe a great deal to my former students who have taught me so much, though I would prefer that they were the chief beneficiaries of our classroom activities.

The Confession by Gramatte'

IN PRINCIPIO ERAT VERBUM

Georges Lemaître, a Catholic abbé and astronomer, earned an important place in the history of science in 1927 when he hypothesized that the universe began when a "primeval atom" of infinite density exploded. He was the first to announce so bold a theory. Predictably, some of his contemporaries ridiculed him, arguing that this theory was nothing more than a transparent ploy to make *Genesis* look scientifically credible.

Lemaître was well aware of the controversial nature of his hypothesis and predicted that the observation of receding galaxies would confirm his claim. If the distance between galaxies is increasing, Lemaître postulated, then everything must have been closer together in the past, and perhaps all together in the beginning. Fellow scientists scoffed at this idea as well.

But in 1929 Edwin Hubble presented to the world evidence that galaxies were indeed rushing away from each other. From that time to the present, most scientists, on the basis comprehensive and accurate explanations gleaned from empirical observations, have become convinced that some sort of Big Bang scenario must have occurred. It is now estimated that approximately 13.3 to 13.9 billion years have elapsed since the initial mega-explosion occurred. Lemaître has been fully exonerated.

The Hubble Space Telescope, named after the prestigious astronomer, has confirmed the existence of some 50 billion galaxies. This figure is truly astonishing and has suggested to some that the universe may be so large as to be infinite. No one knows what lies beyond the furthest galaxies. Some of these galaxies could be more than 12 billion light years away. And since light travels at 186,000 miles per second, it travels 6 trillion miles per year. Thus, the furthest known galaxies may be 12 billion times 6 trillion miles away or 72,000,000,000,000,000,000,000 miles (72 sextillion).

Gregg Easterbrook makes some even more astounding points in his fascinating book, *Beside Still Waters: Searching for Meaning in a World of Doubt* (William Morrow, 1998). If the Big Bang had been slightly less violent, the expansion of the universe would have been less rapid, and would soon have collapsed back on itself. Conversely, if the initial detonation had been slightly more violent, the universe might have dispersed into a cosmic soup too thin for the aggregation of stars. There was little margin for error. The ratio of matter and energy to the volume of space at the moment of the Big Bang had to be, scientists tell us, within about one quadrillionth of one percent of the ideal. In addition, space, at the time of the Big Bang, had to be astonishingly flat for the universe to develop. If it had not, the universe would have come to an end in a small fraction of a second, or would have expanded so rapidly that the universe would have been too cold for stars to form and life to evolve. George Will has commented on this extraordinarily improbable occurrence by stating that "what is is staggeringly implausible, and that is theologically suggestive" (*Newsweek*, November 9, 1998, p. 88).

A good companion to Easterbrook's work is Stephen M. Barr's *Modern Physics and Ancient Faith* (Notre Dame Press, 2003). "Why is the universe so big?" he asks. Thinking on a cosmic scale is indeed mind boggling. It takes 1.5 billion years for life to evolve, he informs us. In that time, the universe has been ever-expanding at a colossal rate. In terms of space, life comes at an enormous price. Man himself, Professor Barr states, however, is just the "right size," which is to say that he is the geometric mean between the size of planet earth and the size of an atom.

Science offers increasingly compelling evidence that the universe evolved not from chaos to order, but from profound principles of order that operated from the very beginning. According to Dr. Barr: the "laws of chemistry are themselves the consequence of the beautifully elaborate laws of electromagnetism and quantum mechanics, which in turn come from the even more profound structures studied in 'quantum field theory.'"

Order precedes chance. The intrinsic order of an atom precedes one atom combining with other atoms. Chance proceeds from order. The question, "What are the chances that life could have evolved from chaos?" is not so much a question than a contradiction. Order, however subtle and small, existed at the outset. The great mathematician and physicist Hermann Weyl avers that "In our knowledge of physical nature we have penetrated so far that we can obtain a vision of the flawless harmony which is in conformity with sublime reason" (*Mind and Nature: Selected Writings on Philosophy, Mathematics and Physics*, Princeton University Press, 2009).

Finally, as astrophysicist Sir James Jeans has remarked, "The universe begins to look more like a great thought than a great machine". Order precedes chance, thought precedes matter, and God the Creator precedes creation. It is not unreasonable, therefore, to assert that behind the "Big Bang" is an intelligent being. *"In principio erat Verbum, et Verbum erat apud Deum, et Deum erat Verbum."*

THE FOUR RIGHTS

C. S. Lewis' *The Four Loves*, which was published in 1960, is a classic. The author succeeded with his accustomed wit and wisdom in showing how four kinds of love—affection, friendship, amorous love, and charity—are both distinctive as well as inter-related. He penned this work just three years before he passed away. Had he lived a little longer he may have bequeathed to our confused world *The Four Rights*.

The four rights that I will attempt to delineate are also both distinctive as well as inter-related. As a method of demonstrating these two characteristics, I have chosen a third person narrative. Let us imagine the evolving life of Thomas who is intimately involved with each of these rights.

First of all, Thomas exists. His existence, the most fundamental act of his being, is the basis for the most elementary of his rights. Since he is, he has a right to be. No one can argue that he does not have such a right. His existence is his greatest gift since he would be nothing without it. Thomas exists and closely tied to his existence is the fact that he is living. He has a right to continue living because he ceases to be if his life is taken from him.

We observe that there is a profound instinct for self-preservation in all men. This instinct not only expresses itself in the desire to go on living but in the desire to develop and grow, forces that are deeply rooted in every human being. Thomas is acutely aware of this instinct, cherishes his existence and want to go on living. His instincts are perfectly natural. Therefore the basis for Thomas' rights to exist and go on living is the natural law. But mere existing and living do not complete Thomas' natural endowment. He also possesses an inclination to do something with his life so that he fulfills himself and advances toward his destiny. Therefore, his natural rights extend to his right to truth, to freedom, and to a knowledge of God. In short, he has a natural right to be fully himself. No one has the right to deny Thomas any of these natural rights.

Thomas becomes educated, earns an advanced degree and applies for a position at a university. He signs a contract with the school's president. He now has, by mutual consent, the right to teach at this particular institution. This is not a natural right, but one that is contractual. If the contract is violated by either party, a legal case may ensue that is adjudicated by a judge. In parts of ancient Greece, a stick was use to represent a binding contract. Each party would retain a piece of the broken stick. The contract could be ratified when the two parts of the stick were reunited. The Greek word *symbolon* is an amalgam of *syn + bole* which means "throwing together". The reunification of the stick would confirm that each party had a contractual right. Today, we understand a "symbol" a something that brings two things together, such as the American flag representing America.

Having his natural rights secured, as well as his contractual right to teach, Thomas enters the class room and speaks to his students. He reminds them that since they have earned their way into his classroom, either by paying tuition or winning a scholarship, they have a right to be taught. This right is neither a natural right nor a contractual right but a claims right. Thomas, must honor their right to be taught by exercising his duty to teach. The students have a claim on their teacher, so to speak, that he teach them. If he fails to exercise his duty, the students as well as the school can take action.

Thomas now begins his first lecture. He asks his students whether they think everyone has a right to marry. He argues that marriage is a conditional right, which is to say that it is dependent on certain conditions being in place. Age, mutual consent, blood relation, sexual differences, and marital status are among these conditions. If these conditions are not met, there is no right to marry. For example, a man does not have the right to marry his daughter.

With regard to all of these rights, there must be a corresponding duty. Thomas has a right to life, but he is not safe unless others honor their duty not to harm him. Parties of a contract must be dutiful to each other. A claims right is meaningless unless someone dutifully fulfills that right. With regard to conditional rights, one has a duty not to violate any of the conditions. Rights and duties, in one way or another, are correlative. There are no rights without the appropriate corresponding duties.

The subject of rights is of critical importance in today's moral climate because there is a clamor to use one kind of right in the place of another and omitting one kind of right altogether. The most egregious example of this relates to abortion. The decision to abort assumes that the right to abortion as well as the right to life of the unborn are conditional. Among these conditions are the will of the mother and the health of the unborn child. In this case, abortion, which violates a natural right, is regarded as exercising a conditional right. In addition, marriage, which is truly a conditional right, is being treated more and more as if it were an absolute right.

Rights and duties are opposite sides of the same coin. In some languages, a single word is used to signify both rights and duties. Of the two, however, it may be argued that duty is more important. Thomas realizes at an early age that he has a duty to make something of his life. As he proceeds, he is met with unjust obstacles that block his development. He then claims that he has a right to be himself and that no one should arbitrarily stand in his way. A court may honor his rights, but only his conscience can activate his duties. We would be wise if we put duty first. We have more control of ourselves than we have of others.

Aeneas Taking Leave of Dido by Romanelli

THE COMPLETE THINKER

"The Complete Thinker" is borrowed from the title of Dale Ahlquist's 2012 book, the subtitle of which is *The Marvelous Mind of G. K. Chesterton*. "Thinking," for Chesterton, "means connecting things". Ahlquist regards G. K.'s thinking as "complete" in the sense that it deals with a wide variety of subjects and integrates them in a consistent pattern. It is as if Chesterton has conducted a symphony in which all the instruments are playing in perfect harmony.

Chesterton credits Catholicism for assisting him in the valuable exercise of thinking. In *The Catholic Church and Conversion* he stated that "To become a Catholic is not to leave off thinking, but to learn how to think." Catholic universities have always stressed the importance of logic which serves as a basis for clear and reliable thinking. There is no limit to where thought can carry us, but its starting point is not whatever one might think it to be. The fact that Einstein could connect the energy locked up in an atom with its mass times the square of the speed of light is a prodigious example of the ability of thought to discover new horizons. The Church loves thinking, properly directed, because it opens new vistas that display the glory of God's creation.

And so, I find it disheartening when I learn that someone has decided to leave the Church on the erroneous belief that She discourages thinking. Let us take but one example (and there are many). In a taped television interview, Steve Allen, a man who displayed his various gifts on television, in motion pictures, as an author, a composer, and pianist, confessed that he left the Catholic Church when he was 30 years of age because "it did all the thinking for you" and he wanted to think things out for himself.

155

His remark is really an insult to every Catholic who remains in the Church. Pascal, Copernicus, Dante, Newman, Mendel, Pasteur, Mauriac, Lemaître, Lejeune, Maritain, and numerous others never felt intellectually stifled because of their membership in the Church. Fr. Vincent McNabb, O.P makes a most pertinent remark in his invaluable little book, *The Catholic Church and Philosophy* when he writes as follows: "The peculiar function of the Catholic Church in the story of our civilization has been to preserve the philosophic conquests of pagan antiquity and to expand them over an even greater range of discovery than the greatest of the ancients had commanded."

One might stress the significance of the word discovery. There are worlds yet to be discovered through thinking. But it is not easy to be a complete thinker. Freud new something about science but nothing about man's spiritual nature. Marx knew about social structures but had no regard for the dignity of the individual. Rousseau believed in the General Will, but not in the particular thought. Nietzsche was infatuated by the superman, but rejected God. Sartre extolled freedom, but his philosophy had little to say about responsibility. Comte praised abstract humanity, but had little regard for anyone who believed in a higher power. Many of the thinkers whose thought shaped the modern world were not "complete thinkers". Their thought remained incomplete, failing to be applicable to the many realms that make up reality.

We all need help no matter what endeavor or activity we pursue. An opera singer needs a mentor, an athlete needs a coach, a student need a teacher, a dancer need an instructor, and a child needs a parent. To begin the challenging art of thinking by oneself, unaided by the wisdom of the ages, is bound to fail at some point. Chesterton was very severe on this point. "Thinking in isolation and with pride," he remarked, "ends in being an idiot."

The one philosopher, more than any other, who placed his hope in solitary thinking is Rene Descartes. His famous phrase, "I think therefore I am," did not inaugurate a new philosophy, but terminated it. It died the moment it was born because it could not make the connection between thought and reality. His thinking affirmed his own being but could not cross over and affirm anyone else's. His philosophy logically ended in solipsism, the strange view that only the thinker has real existence. Alexis de Tocqueville made the comment, in his classic *Democracy in America*, that all Americans are Cartesians, even though none of them have read Descartes. Cartesianism is in the air and is highly infectious. The notion that I can produce my own philosophy from my own solitary starting point is pandemic.

Jacques Maritain has made reference to this problem. In *The Dream of Descartes* he states that "Every modern philosopher is a Cartesian in the sense that he looks upon himself as starting off in the absolute, and as having the mission of bringing men a new conception of the world." To be a realistic thinker, one must be aware of the traps. The Church helps us to identify the traps and keep us on the right course. The Church is *Magister*.

Returning to Steve Allen, that wonderfully charming host of the first Tonight Show.  After he left the Church he identified himself as a "humanist". And for his humanistic efforts he received many awards from various humanist societies. The essential problem with "humanism," however, despite its universal sounding name, is that it does not include all humans. It excludes, for example, orthodox Catholics who have a broader and more inclusive view of human beings. Catholics believe that all human beings have infinite value and are equally loved by God. Here is an example of what Dale Ahlquist means by being a "complete thinker". Thinking is not complete if it purports to include everyone, and yet excludes probably more than it includes.

E. F. Schumacher's *Guide for the Perplexed* is a modern version of the one Moses Maimonides wrote back in the twelfth century by that same title. We are all, to a certain extent, perplexed. Therefore, we need help. The Church will not abandon us. We must be wary, however, not to abandon the Church.

Harvest of Our Mere Humanism Years by Kurelek

A NOTE OF GOOD NEWS

Hostility against pro-life students on college campuses has been escalating. This is not only troubling, but difficult to comprehend. Abortion is a violent act that ends an innocent life. It is, as a matter of fact, the country's most egregious act of domestic violence. Why, then, is so much animus directed against students who stand opposed to abortion. Secondly, since colleges are mandated to be educational centers where dialogue and debate are an integral part, why is there such opposition to freedom of speech when it centers on defending life?

But there is a note of good news. A federal court has ordered Gregory Thatcher, a professor of public health at Fresno State, to pay $17,000 in damages to Fresno Students of Life for violating their free speech rights. He is also ordered to undergo First Amendment training. This is a victory not only for pro-life students, but for education as well as the United States Constitution.

Thatcher himself, together with at least seven of his students whom he recruited, erased chalk messages that the Fresno students of Life had written. When the students informed Thatcher that they had been given permission to state their messages, he proceeded to rub out one of the messages with his shoe while stating, "You have permission to put [the chalk messages] down . . . I have permission to get rid of it." The disagreement in this instance, however, was not merely between two parties (with one dominating the other), but between Thatcher and the United States Constitution. The rights that are guaranteed by the Constitution cannot be violated arbitrarily by recalcitrant individuals. Thatcher, by defying the law of the land, is inviting chaos, a curious stance for a professor of public health.

Travis Barham, legal counsel representing Alliance Defending Freedom, spoke in behalf of the students: "No public university professor has the authority to silence any student speech he happens to find objectionable or to recruit other students to participate in his censorship." Kristan Hawkins, who is the president of Students for Life of America hailed the Court's decision as "a victory for all students who have the same Constitutional rights as professors." She went on to say that "nationwide we are seeing incredible opposition to pro-life speech as our student leaders and volunteers speak for the defenseless, reach out to pregnant women, and educate on the violence of abortion. But as this case illustrates, we are not going to be silent, even if it takes going to court."

This case brings to mind the question of the quality of education in America. Various ideologies — feminist, Marxist, that of the LGBTQ, *etc.* — have been displacing a proper education of American history. In one history text, 14 pages are devoted to feminism, while George Washington is given but a single page. Philosophy, as the love of wisdom, is systematically replaced by relativism, skepticism, deconstruction, or even nihilism. Totalitarianism is routinely indoctrinated, although presented under the auspices of diversity. To complain about any of this often has dire consequences for the student. Hence, many assume a passive role and lose their incentive to search for meaning.

Students, who usually pay a great deal of money for an education often find themselves torn between conforming to an ideology or struggling to secure their rights as citizens. Thus far, students who defend life are waging a lonely battle. They should be joined by "students for an education," "students for America," "students for civil rights," and other such groups. The tide may be turning, but there is a long way to go. Education should be liberating, not a source of shame and an occasion for vindictiveness. We applaud the pro-life students at Fresno State and hope that their courageous actions are an inspiration for others and a lesson for those who need to be taught.

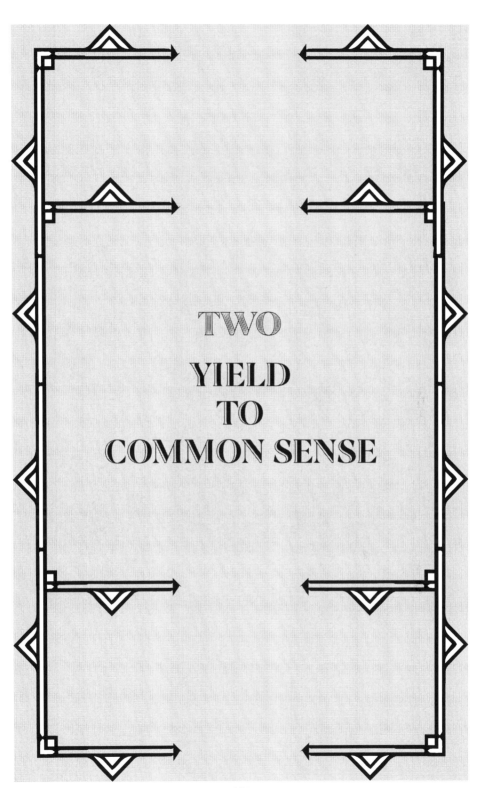

TWO
YIELD TO COMMON SENSE

DOES COMMON SENSE HAVE A FUTURE?

In an anthology entitled, *The Future of Thomism,* the distinguished Thomistic philosopher Josef Pieper observes that "There is something peculiar and even strange in the situation of philosophy today." It is as if, Pieper asks, reflecting the prevailing mood of contemporary scepticism, "Why philosophy at all?" G. K. Chesterton, a few years earlier made a similar observation about the virtual disappearance of philosophy: "Since the modern world began in the sixteenth century, nobody's system of philosophy has really corresponded to everybody's sense of realty; to what, if left to themselves, common men wold call common sense."

Both Chesterton and Pieper are lamenting the sharp decline of a philosophy that begins with common sense, one congruent with that of St. Thomas Aquinas which, as G. K. tersely states, "stands founded on the universal common conviction that eggs are eggs." The modern thinker looks at the world as if it is a gigantic masquerade party in which nothing is what it seems to be. Eggs are not simply eggs but disguises for something else which is also a disguise. Once all the disguises are removed, nothing is left. In short, deconstruction leads directly to nihilism; common sense is replaced by uncommon nonsense.

The question "does Thomism have a future" is intimately related to the question, "Does common sense have a future?" In the absence of a philosophy that begins with common sense, what Aquinas refers to as "the authority of the senses," an intellectual vacuum is created. Just as nature abhors a vacuum, so does the mind. Deconstruction, however, is not so much a replacement for philosophy, but an opposition to it. Therefore, deconstruction is an anti-philosophy.

We need philosophy to understand the nature of things. If we do not know the nature of things we will not know their value, and how they should be used. Such knowledge is required if we have any hope of being just. In the contemporary world deconstruction has taken dead aim at sex, marriage, and the family, which underscore the supreme importance of a philosophy that can recognize what things really are. We can allude to three areas in particular that deconstruction seeks to take apart.

1) It is assumed, after millennia of acceptance, that the male/female dichotomy is not at all natural but something that is socially constructed. Feminist Julia Kristeva, for example, argues that there are no women, though we should keep the word since it provides them with political benefits. After dismissing common sense, contradictions are welcomed. The traditional notions of man and woman as distinctive, therefore, are to be regarded as stereotypes or myths. *Genesis*  is not the Word of God, but an example of a text that must be deconstructed. If philosophy does not begin with wonder, it must begin with arrogance.

2) Closely connected with the deconstruction of male and female, is the deconstruction of the terms mother, father, husband, and wife, as well as son, daughter, and grandchildren. Generic terms such as parent, spouse, or progenitor may be used in their place. Marriage, therefore, should avoid atavistic standards of heteronormativity so that it can be more free, more empowering, and more inclusive. It is believed that this free-wheeling approach will be beneficial for everyone.

3) Also, closely allied with the above categories, are the social roles that have been assigned to men and women in the past. These roles include occupations, attire, customs, language and behavior. This far-sweeping deconstruction represents a complete revolution in society, although deconstructionists themselves allegedly oppose socially constructed projects. Paragraph 9 of the draft *Platform For Action for Beijing* at the 1990 International Conference on Women reads as follows: "Nothing short of a radical transformation of the relationships between men and women will enable to world to meet challenges of new the new millennium."

Deconstructionists want to obliterate all differences between people because they believe that difference means inequality and that inequality means exploitation. Consequently, they find the concept of complementarity anathema. Nonetheless, it is the complementarity between the sexes that makes it possible for human life to continue. Neither "men" nor "women" alone can procreate. Men and women are not the same biologically, and no amount of socially conditioning can alter that fact. The deconstruction of nature to raw putty in the hands of deconstructionists can lead only to social chaos.

Norman Mailer has made the comment in one of his many books, that if he ever meets St. Thomas Aquinas in the next world, he will commend him for "That most excellent phrase . . . the authority of the senses". Mailer is also commending all those philosophers who stubbornly hold to the notion that it is through our senses (not through our dreams) that we come in contact with reality.

The deconstruction of nature must also include the deconstruction of human nature. For anyone of common sense, however, this is a most desperate and futile project. At the beginning of his longest encyclical, *Fides et Ratio*, Saint John Paul II draws attention to the sheer naturalness of philosophizing. In every culture, he points out, human beings ask the fundamental questions: "Who am I? Where have I come from and where am I going? Why is there evil? What is there after this life?" To suppress these questions is to suppress humanity. Nonetheless, deconstructionists will argue that there is no such thing as humanity.

How did society lose its respect for common sense? Samuel Taylor Coleridge once remarked that "Common sense in an uncommon degree  is what the world calls wisdom." We may also add that wisdom is also in short supply. Society is in love with novelty and there is nothing novel about common sense. It is also infatuated with change, an attitude that disparages what is stable and even necessary. And its love affair with what is trendy often obscures what is a permanent possession. Academia tells us to rid ourselves of the "hegemonic taxonomy of bourgeois heteronormativity," which simply means, "scrap the male-female distinction". An old adage is need here: "One pound of learning requires ten pounds of common sense to apply it."

CLARITY IN A TIME OF CHAOS

The year 1938 was a year of global turmoil. Hitler had seized control of the German army and placed Nazis in key posts. The civil war in Spain continued unabated on its path of murderous violence. Benito Mussolini published an anti-Jewish/African manifesto. Winston Churchill condemned Hitler's annexation of Czechoslovakia. The League of Nations declared Japan to be an aggressor against China. It was a year in which certain political factions declared that Jews, Africans, Spaniards, Czechs, and Chinese were not fully human.

Yet, in this year of turbulence, there were areas that remained unaffected. In 1938, the beginning of human life was not an issue that was caught up in the maelstrom of cultural confusion. There was no reason to distort or contaminate its scientifically documentable reality. And so, Margaret Shea Gilbert, though a name that is not remembered by many, wrote a small book entitled *Biography of the Unborn* in which she described, with grace and biological precision, the beginning of human life.

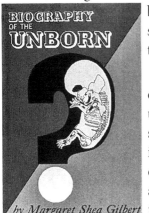

"Life begins for each of us," she wrote in her opening paragraph, "at an unfelt, unknown, and unhonoured instant when a minute, wriggling sperm plunges into a mature ovum or egg . . . It is at this moment of fusion of the sperm and the ovum (a process call fertilization) that there arises a new individual who contains the potentialities for unnumbered generations of men."

The general public looked favorably on Gilbert's book. It was not controversial in the least. The Williams & Wilkins Company, a leading publisher of scientific and medical works at the time, honored it by awarding its author a prize of $1,000 for "the best book on a scientific subject for general reading". Ten years after its initial printing, Readers' Digest widened the book's readership by publishing it in a condensed form. 1938 was an island of serenity concerning the origin of human life despite what was going on in the rest of the world.

The fertilized egg, or zygote, contains all the information it needs to direct its development to the point where it attains consciousness and resembles other adult human beings. World class geneticist Jérôme Lejeune, the discoverer of trisomy, has stated that "as no other information will enter later into the zygote, the fertilized egg, one is forced to admit that all the necessary and sufficient information to define that particular creature is found at fertilization." The zygote's end is implicit in its beginning. Human life, therefore, begins at fertilization.

There is a widespread presumption that science marches on quite independently of culture influence. This view is naïve in the extreme, as history has shown. One need only consider the immense political pressure placed on scientists in Nazi Germany and in Stalinist Russia to subordinate their scientific findings to politically correct viewpoints to confirm this assertion. Science may go forwards, but it also can go backwards.

Justice Oliver Wendell Holmes said it well in his treatise, Medical Essays, in the mid-19th Century, when he remarked that "medicine, professedly founded on observation, is as sensitive to outside influence, political, religious, philosophical, imaginative, as is the barometer to the atmospheric density." In theory, he said, medicine "ought to go on its own straightforward inductive path," but in practice there exists "a closer relation between the Medical Sciences and the conditions of Society and the general thought of the time, than would at first be expected." He was writing not only about medicine, but about science in general.

The general thought in the present is not congenial to the scientific basis for the beginning of human life. Some embryologists have accepted the fictitious and unscientific notion of a "pre-embryo" to make it appear that life did not begin at the moment of fertilization but at some indeterminate time later. The need to rationalize abortion has led to a falsification of science.

American biologists, in general, were more free in 1938 to expound upon the beginning of life than they are in today's climate. 1938 was a turbulent year in many ways, but in that year the science of embryology that pinpointed the origin of human life was allowed to proceed according to its own objective standards. That same climate also allowed people to read about the origin of human life without fear of being out of step with the regnant attitudes of the times. We would all prefer clarity to chaos. Unfortunately, it is chaos that often makes it extremely difficult to find clarity. The year 1938 has much to teach us.

Behold Man Without God by Kurelek

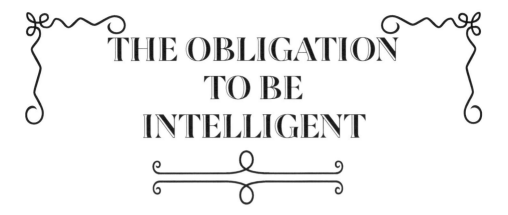

THE OBLIGATION TO BE INTELLIGENT

Intelligence is very much like water. It does not have much pizazz but just as water is necessary to sustain life, intelligence is necessary to sustain a moral life. Intelligence in action is quiet, hardly noticeable, and certainly not newsworthy. By contrast, protest has all the opposite features. It is clamorous, attention-getting, and eminently newsworthy. Protest, apart from the object against which it is directed, also has great appeal to the protestor. Protesting often flatters the protestor as bold, adventurous, righteous, and a champion of freedom. The personally exhilarating aspects of protesting, therefore, may obscure whether or not the protest is truly an expression of intelligence.

People in America have a constitutional right to protest. But they cannot be protesting all the time. Intelligence, on the other hand, is something that is always with us and can be called upon at any time and under any circumstances. It is also a universal faculty and is a basis for universal agreement. This is because the natural object of intelligence is truth which is the common unifier of all men. Just as scientists can use their intelligence to agree on the orderly movement of planets, so too, intelligence can guide people in living an orderly life.

It is only too evident that many forms of protest are loosely, if at all, connected with intelligence. An LGBT transgendered activist is currently protesting the fact that the British Columbia Human Rights Tribunal has referred to this person as "born a male". We think of self-immolation, streaking, hunger strikes, various forms of violence, or the refusal to honor the Stars and Stripes at an athletic contest. A situation exists at the moment in which National Football players are protesting President Trump's protest that they should not be seen as protesting the American flag. At this point the primary reason for protesting is lost on the battlefield of competing protests. Death threats have been reported.

The key point here is that protests, laudable and righteous as they may seem to be, must always be subordinated to intelligence. The notion of being subordinated to anything may not appeal to every protestor. After all, the protestor may regard himself as representing a higher vision. He may even enjoy the role of being an insubordinate.

Philosophy, which is not nearly as newsworthy as protesting, if it is to be of any value, must subordinate itself to truth. Paradoxically, it is only by subordinating oneself to truth that one can find freedom. If the key is to unlock the door, it must be subordinated to the structure of the lock. If the liberal arts are to liberate us, we must first learn about the nature of the human being and what people must do in order to achieve peace and prosperity. A worthwhile form of protest, then, would be to protest the separation of protesting from the overarching significance of truth. This, however, is a form of protest that has yet to capture the interest of the Mass Media.

We have a right to protest, but, more significantly, we have an obligation to be intelligent. It is the use of intelligence that ensures that a protest is justifiable. This means nothing to the hordes of professional protestors who are bussed in to join a protest, blissfully unconcerned about the rectitude of the protest. A protest can easily take on the form of a "happening," calling attention to nothing other than itself. It is unfortunate that such protests can give a bad name to protests, and society does need worthwhile protests. The words of the distinguished social philosopher Yves Simon come to mind: "That society is blessed whose aspirations coincide with truth." Legitimate protests can assist in the realization of those aspirations.

A protest that is severed from truth is highly susceptible to being incorporated into an ideology. Abortion advocates have created an ideology that disconnects itself from truth and attacks those who defend life. Hence, expressions such as "curb your dogma" and "get your rosaries off our ovaries" disparage Catholics while placing abortion in a narrow ideology that rejects any intelligent discussion of the issue. They speak of "rights" but not of truth.

I recall the difficulty I had trying to make the case for the use of intelligence to a group of ideological feminists who were more passionate about their "rights". They would insist, for example, that they had a "right" to wear any kind of attire they so pleased and would not compromise their hard fought freedom by capitulating to anyone who told them how they should dress. I would try to explain that intelligence has the wonderful advantage of anticipating consequences. A woman may dress in a provocative way and then be offended by those whom she provokes. But the use of intelligence looks beyond mere rights so that unwanted results to not transpire. A person has a right to own a bicycle, I would say. But this right all by itself does not safeguard it from being stolen. If you leave your bicycle on the front lawn, unlocked and unattended, someone will eventually steal it. Intelligence would direct you to hide the bicycle in a proper place when you are not using it. The use of intelligence in this regard is far more beneficial than the assertion of rights. Ideologies, unhappily, sometimes have no room for either intelligence or truth.

Prisoner Solzhenitsyn

Intelligence is inalienable. Even in a highly restrictive society where protests are not allowed, we can still utilize our intelligence. It is a faculty that cannot be taken from us. Alexander Solzhenitsyn never surrendered the use of his intelligence, even while living under the most degrading circumstances in the Gulag. He committed his intelligence to posterity through the written word. Therefore, it is especially unfortunate when we deprive ourselves of its use.

The comparison between intelligence and water, made at the outset, bears a comparison between a line from Samuel Taylor Coleridge's *Rime of the Ancient Mariner*, "Water, water, everywhere and not a drop to drink," and the present inapplicability of intelligence: "Intelligence, intelligence everywhere, and no one wants to think."

Oh, to be torn twixt love and duty

IN DEFENSE OF DUTY

The aftermath of America's deadliest shooting in Las Vegas has brought to light many acts of heroism between strangers. I found one extraordinary act in particular of special interest. A woman chose to stay with a dying man for four hours. Something deep inside her told her that she could not allow another person, even one who was a complete stranger, to die alone. This was a more intensely human act than that of the Good Samaritan, though one consistent with this great parable. A person who is dying can evoke in us our deepest solicitude. This woman felt it was her solemn duty to attend to this man. She could not abandon him to die without the comfort of another human being.

Some may object that the word "duty" does not do justice to such a generous and heroic act. We often think of duty in terms of drudgery. Cleaning the house, making beds, raking the yard, doing the dishes are various duties we are often reluctant to perform. But these are duties on a lower plane. We have a duty to our neighbor that operates on a moral, even Christian level. The Russian existentialist philosopher Nikolai Berdyaev has remarked that "Our attitude to all men would be Christian if we regarded them as though they were dying, and determine our relation to them in the light of death, both their and our own death. A person who is dying calls forth a special kind of feeling. Our attitude to him is at once softened and lifted to a higher plane."

We hear far more talk about "rights" than about "duties". This is a point that is made abundantly evident in Mary Ann Glendon's award winning book, *Rights Talk*. We assert our rights, but must perform our duties. Hence, our rights do not cost us anything. Our duties can be onerous. Yet duty is more profound than rights. Duties can be the correlatives of rights. A student who pays his tuition has a right to learn. Therefore, the teacher has a corresponding duty to teach. Parents have the duty to care for their children who, in turn have the right to care. Nonetheless, there are duties for which there are no corresponding rights. A dying person does not have the right to be attended to by a stranger. Here is where duty transcends rights and through the generosity of one's being a person does what needs to be done without having any regard to satisfying a right, his own or anyone else's. Such generosity, as Jacques Maritain states, springs from the "deepest requirements of being, those through which beings resemble God".

Duty also precedes rights. We may have a right to be happy, but we will not achieve that goal if we do not perform our duty. The Indian poet, Rabindranath Tagore has captured this notion beautifully when he writes as follows: "I slept and dreamed that life was joy. I awakened and saw that life was duty and behold, duty was joy." The historian of philosophy, Will Durant, has said something similar: "Never mind your happiness; do you duty." Happiness is something that "happens" when we have fulfilled our duty.

We are asleep to the moral order when we naively believe that life owes us happiness. The fact that there is so much unhappiness in the world is a clear indication that happiness is not as readily possessed as picking apples from an apple tree. "Happiness was born a twin," said Robert Browning, meaning that happiness cannot be a private possession. "It is not good for man to be alone." In order to be happy, we must involves ourselves with others. Our duty to serve the good of our neighbor is antecedent to happiness. Duty comes first. Our reluctance to do our duty is the key to understanding the unhappy state of mankind.

Duties are more profound than rights because they more faithfully characterize the essence of the human being as generous, loving, and one who is destined to serve others. We were born to fulfill our duty through love. Rights, important as they are, are more of a legal concept. Duty is rooted in our being. On the other hand, rights are more profound with regard to God since He has the right (and not the duty) to create us by virtue of His divine prerogative. God is also just, which means that He owes it to Himself to give His creatures what they require by their nature. Man has his duties; God has His rights. The correspondence between Divine Right and human duty may very well capture the essential drama of the creation of man and his return to God.

Carolers Heading to Church by Kurelek

Prairie Pirate Ship by Kurelek

IDEALS AND FANTASIES

Philosophy cannot get off the ground without making distinctions. According to the scholastic maxim, *Philosophi est distinguere*. That something either is or it is not is a most fundamental distinction without which we are not able to think coherently. Quite often, however, in order to define things clearly, one distinction requires further distinctions.

And so it is with distinguishing an ideal from a fantasy. The Irish novelist and philosopher, Dame Jean Iris Murdoch expresses concisely how I would like to use the word 'fantasy' in this essay when she complains that "We live in a fantasy world, a world of illusion. The great task in life is to find reality." The great physicist, Albert Einstein, captures how I employ the word 'ideal" when he states that "The ideals that have lighted my way, and time after time have given me new courage to face life cheerfully, have been Kindness, Beauty, and Truth."

The term 'ideal' is sometimes used to indicate something that is wholly unattainable. We can distinguish, then, between an ideal that is unattainable and unrealistic form one that is both attainable (at least in part) as well as realistic. Therefore, we can speak of an 'ideal' as an aspect of reality which, when attained, is personally fulfilling. At the same time, the term 'fantasy' can refer to the fanciful expressions of reality provided by such eminent writers as J. R. R. Tolkien and C. S. Lewis. A fantasy can enlighten one to the truth of things or it can wander off into the realm of the illusory. Politics is too often nothing more than a fantasy in the latter sense.

G. K. Chesterton neatly contrasts the practicality of ideals with the impracticality of politics in his book *Orthodoxy*. In so doing, he is turning the conventional world on its head: "They said that I should lose my ideals and begin to believe in the methods of practical politicians. Now, I have not lost my ideals in the least; my faith in fundamentals is exactly what it always was. What I have lost is my childlike faith in practical politics."

Because it is so easy, as well as commonplace, to confuse the terms 'ideal' and 'fantasy', people often find themselves pursuing a fantasy when they assume that they are pursuing a worthy ideal. This confusion, for people who may be well intentioned, provides a situation that calls for much tolerance and sympathy. Struggling to make things better is a noble endeavor. The critical point, however, is to make sure that the struggle is for an ideal that is fulfilling and not a fantasy that will prove disappointing. Here is an issue that has the potential of transforming mere acquaintances into friends.

We have a natural inclination to strive to achieve an ideal that will make the world a better place. George W. Bush once remarked that "We are bound by things of the spirit — by shared commitments to common ideals." He envisioned this human condition as illuminating the way for all Americans to achieve unity. His reference to the notion that we are "bound by things of the spirit" is consistent with the Vatican II injunction "that all men should be at once impelled by nature and also bound by a moral obligation to seek the truth (*Gaudium et Spes*)." A true ideal has its counterpart in the nature of the human being. Ideals are worth striving for because they are enriching. On the other hand, there is nothing within us that inclines us in the direction of pure fantasies.

Abortion, euthanasia, and the LGBTQ agenda attract people's enthusiasms. But they are not ideals to which anyone should commit themselves. It is fantastical to think that their implementation will bring about a better world. Abortion claims roughly 40 million lives each year throughout the world. Euthanasia is expanding its frontier so that it is now claiming the lives of children. Approximately 35 million people throughout the globe have died of AIDS related illnesses and 34 million people currently have the HIV virus. Even a spokesperson for LGBTQ lamented that "Our lifestyle had become an elaborate suicide ritual." True ideals should be rooted in our common human nature. They are for everyone. Our fantasies, on the other hand, are rooted in our private dreams.

Exchanging a fantasy for an ideal would constitute a major revolution in a person's life. Energy and dedication are simply not enough. What we hold sacred is critical. Ultimately, the ideals of peace, goodness, beauty, justice, and truth are personified in God. God is also the God of Life. Therefore, in directing our efforts to any of the divine attributes, we are also directing our energies to both God and to the Life that He represents.

We should aspire to things that are at the same time both above us and within us. This is implied in the adage, "Hitch your wagon to a star". Ideals must unite heaven and earth. We are all possessors of a religious impulse. But which God should we serve? Should it be the God of Life or the god of convenience? This is an old Biblical question. And herein lies the critical difference between a true and realistic ideal and a misleading and fraudulent fantasy.

Dogs or People by Kurelek

Horse and Train by Alex Colville

THREE

THE
RIGHT OF WAY

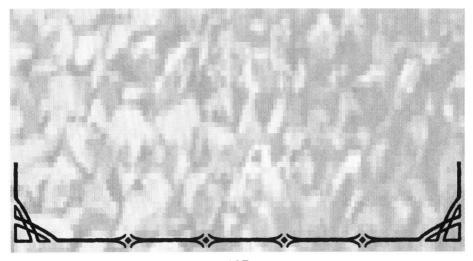

Christ Preaching by Rembrandt

IN PRAISE OF CLARITY

A hostess sent out party invitations to her friends that requested RSVPs. When she received a completely illegible response from a particular doctor, she asked her husband what she should do. Upon his advice, she brought the indecipherable letter to a druggist since members of the pharmaceutical profession are reputed to be experts in decoding bad handwriting. The druggist studied the letter for a moment, excused himself, and returned after a few minutes with a small package. "Here you are," said the druggist cheerfully. "That will be $125.50, please."

For many Catholics these days, it's not difficult for them to preserve the essence of this comedy of errors while changing the identities of the players. The doctor is replaced by a Bishop while a parish priest fills in for the druggist. The distraught woman is the typical confused Catholic layperson.

The point here is that when things are not made clear, we may wind up paying a high price, monetarily or otherwise, for something that we do not want and do not need. When it comes to making our thoughts clear, we cannot be too careful. In Italian, the word *tradutore* means "translator," while the word *traditore* refers to a "traitor". The Bible needs translators, not traitors, though the latter have, upon occasion, supplanted the former. In 1631, a printing of the King James Bible went horribly astray when the verse "Thou shalt not commit adultery" was misprinted as "Thou shalt commit adultery." For the want of a three-letter negative, an altogether different message was communicated. The printers were fined £300, which was an exceedingly large sum at the time, and most of the copies were recalled and burned. This wayward edition, as the result of a single typo, came to be known as 'The Wicked Bible' or 'The Sinners' Bible'.

In the early Church, a bitter controversy arose concerning how to understand the relationships between the members of the Holy Trinity. A single letter, an *iota*, the smallest letter in the Greek alphabet, divided two groups of theologians. Some preferred to the term *homoiousios* (*homoios* = similar + *ousia* = substance) which means "of similar substance" to describe the distinctions between the three persons of the Blessed Trinity. Athanasius adopted the term *homoousios*, (*homo* = the same + *ousia* + substance) meaning "of the same substance," which survives as the correct teaching and is recited during the Mass in the Nicene Creed. Thus, a contentious matter was clarified. Put simply, the Father, Son, and Holy Spirit are not merely similar to each other, but are of the same substance. Therefore, God is One, though at the same time Triune. Clarity can be achieved, but it sometimes requires a protracted struggle.

Council of Nicea

Church teaching, especially on moral issues, has always been consistently clear. Abortion is wrong, and so is suicide, adultery, slander, and blasphemy. We need to be clear about what is right and what is wrong so that we can dedicate ourselves to doing what is right and avoid the indignity that goes with doing what is wrong. When we are fuzzy about moral issues, we may choose what we will soon regret. One way in which the Church expresses Her charity is by the clarity of Her teaching.

G. K. Chesterton was a man who constantly strove to achieve clarity. His determination in this regard was no doubt abetted by the fact that foggy notions were very popular even in his day. He denounced as "mere weak-mindedness" the modern habit of saying 'This is my opinion, but I may be wrong'" and the "modern habit of saying 'Everyman has a different philosophy; this is my philosophy and it suits me.'" A person's commitment to clarity is not mitigated by the fear of offending someone or the fear of appearing to be a know-it-all. It overcomes such fears because clarity of expression is simply more important than such disabling fears. When we are clear, we know where we stand. And in knowing where we stand, we are in a better position to know how we are to live. We may not be clear about everything, but we should strive to clear whenever we can. Intentional cloudiness is not a virtue.

Abraham Lincoln would undoubtedly have been surprised to learn that some of his speeches came to be honored as great literature. His aim was simply to communicate clearly and convincingly. And this his did with superlative mastery, as notably exemplified by his *Gettysburg Address* ("That government of the people, by the people, for the people, shall not perish from the earth."). His messages were sufficiently clear that millions of his fellow citizens could make them their own. Moreover, he did not cower in the midst of controversy: "As I would not be a slave, so I would not be a master. This expresses my idea of democracy. Whatever differs from this, to the extent of the difference, is no democracy." Lincoln made it abundantly clear what he meant by democracy.

We can hide behind ambiguity, like the Oracle at Delphi, or bury ourselves under an avalanche of high sounding phrases, as academics often do. It takes courage to be clear for it reveals something of ourselves. But clarity is also charity for it provides enlightenment for others.

Return of the Prodigal Son by Murillo

THE IMPORTANCE OF PLACING SECOND

The second, to be mathematically precise, is the time required for a cesium-133 atom to complete 9,192,631,770 oscillations. A lot more can happen within a second than most people realize. Science's notion of exactitude, however, has little in common with the ordinary man's understanding of life. Fascinating as this fact is, as well as completely beyond human comprehension, the duration of the second is not the subject of this essay, but "second" referring to coming after first (from the Latin *sequor*: "I follow").

In his book, *What's Wrong with the World*, G. K. Chesterton refers to the principle of the second wind. "In everything worth having," he writes, "even in every pleasure, there comes a point or tedium that must be survived, so that the pleasure may revive and endure." The joy of learning comes after the boredom of studying; the elation of victory comes after the tedium of training; and the success in business comes after the drudgery of labor. We should not quit on anything before we catch that second wind that will get us over the hump.

In sports, we admire the athlete who makes that critical second effort that is needed to secure a rebound in basketball or when a runner turns on the after-burners and speeds from first to third on a single in baseball. The primary effort is expected, but it is often that second effort that makes the difference between winning and losing. Just as the second wind requires persistence, the second effort presupposes determination. It is the will to continue that demands virtue, not so much the first attempt.

According to the adage, "everyone deserves a second chance". Here, the virtue of forgiveness comes into play. It is unrealistic to expect people to refrain from making mistakes. We all find ourselves in a situation where we need a second chance to amend things or to straighten out our lives.

The second chance allows for atonement. It gives us hope. It relieves us from the pressure of doing everything right the first time. Theologically, we never run out of second chances with God, only time.

Blessed are the poor because they appreciate the value of things that are second hand. Second hand clothes and second hand books are the affordable possessions of the needy and the curious. They can be as serviceable as their counterparts that are owned for the first-time. They represent values that endure rather than items that must be discarded. There are a tribute to the resourcefulness of their owners. Second hand means second rate only to the fastidious.

The second look is usually a complement. We will never be remembered if we are brushed off with a momentary look. On the other hand, we stand to miss something important when we fail to give it a second look. If love does not flower at first sight, perhaps it needs a second look. The idea that we have only one chance to make a first impression is highly misleading. Our second chance gives us a better chance to make a lasting impression. In Johann Strauss' *Die Fledermaus*, Adele sings, "Look me over once. Look me over twice. You will not remain in the dark." No one wants to be dismissed with a glance. The essence of Jerry Seinfeld's comedy lies in the fact that he is willing to look over what most people overlook.

Perhaps the most important in our inventory of things coming in second is the second thought. This has special significance in the world of philosophy. There is no philosophy, however impoverished, that is devoid of any connection whatsoever with truth. What is wrong with a bad philosophy is always what is omitted. Pro-abortionists rally around a philosophy of choice. Naturally, human beings need to make choices and it would be inhuman to deny them the capacity to choose. Nonetheless, a second thought would indicate that not all choices are good. Consequently, choices should be ordered to what is good, and killing the unborn is hardly a good, nor is larceny, forgery, and other villainies. Choice, therefore, is an incomplete philosophy because it omits the notion of good which is needed to morally validate choice.

It is rather impetuous to find a single partial truth and then elevate it into a philosophy. Choice alone cannot be a philosophy. The search for wisdom needs more than one thought. Rights should not be separated from duties, nor should liberty be severed from responsibility. Dostoevsky talked about how a university student (Raskolnikov, for example, in *Crime and Punishment*) can have his mind infected by incomplete ideas that float on the wind. The second thought is also important in human relations. We rush to judgment if all we have is an initial thought about another person. The second thought introduces additional truths that might change one's perception of the other as well as one's judgment. Second thoughts are also needed in order to have time to think about the possible inadequacy of one's first thought. Thinking is necessary, but it should not be shut down prematurely. Justice to others as well as justice to philosophy take time and therefore must enlist many second thoughts.

Eve was the second sex in the order of creation. This, however, is no indication of any kind of inferiority. She was fashioned, as *Genesis* informs us, from human substance, whereas Adam was created from dust. In addition, Eve was spared the "cosmic loneliness," to cite the expression used by John Paul II in his "Theology of the Body," that Adam suffered. She was made from a human and born directly into a human relationship. Unlike Adam, she did not need to serve an apprenticeship as a gardener or a zoo keeper.

Finally, we think of the second person of the Blessed Trinity who takes on flesh and lives among human beings, precisely as a human being. Arriving second has its values, something about which a good parliamentarian could doff his hat and say in a loud voice: "I second that".

From The Quiet Man

A MODESTY PROPOSAL

Moral virtues are good habits that make us strong. Virtues are to the person what nutrition is to the body. "Empowerment" has become a buzz word for radical feminists who want to become strong. Yet, they often go about shunning what truly makes them strong—virtue—in the interest of pursuing a form of liberation that actually liberates them from virtue and the empowerment it provides.

One example in particular stands out: the rejection of modesty in the interest of freedom. Wendy Shalit reminds us, in her book, *A Return to Modesty: Discovering the Lost Virtue* (1999), that modesty is not prudery, but a natural instinct, and one that can save us from ourselves. She cites some authors who argue that modesty is an invented virtue that should be deconstructed, and others who contend that modesty is unnatural and serves only to discourage women from dressing whichever way they desire. Indeed, modesty is not prudery, but prudence.

The plain truth is that modesty is a fact of life. Madonna, Lady Gaga, Miley Cyrus and many others have made careers out of being purposely and blatantly immodest. In so behaving, they are decidedly not good role models. Nonetheless, their influence is considerable. They know exactly what they are doing and cashing in on presenting themselves as sex objects. Shock sells. Virtue must be pursued.

Modesty in attire, is the way men and women present themselves to others as persons and not as objects. It is both affirmative of personality and protective against exploitation. In this way, modesty is a source of strength. It is also a natural invitation to a person-to-person relationship. The "I-Thou" relationship is infinitely more rewarding than that of the "I-It" relationship.

I recall, with some degree of dismay, trying to make this point in class to a group of feminists. They vehemently insisted that women should have the freedom to dress in any manner they so choose and that men should continue to look at them respectfully. They preferred freedom over virtue even though the freedom they espoused made them vulnerable, whereas a proper modesty would have given them both strength and protection. Their attitude toward men was naïve. They believed that the opposite sex should respond primarily to a feminist ideology rather to a provocative looking female. Men, however, are not disembodied creatures. This feminist disregard for how they look and what they provoke did not empower, but endangered them. Feminism is not always congenial to feminists.

Anne Maloney is an Associate Professor of Philosophy at the College of St. Catherine in St. Paul Minnesota. In an article entitled, *What the Hook-up Culture Has Done to Women* (*Crisis*, June 14, 2016), she bemoans the fact that so many women, tossing modesty aside, have become victims of male lust. After thirty years of teaching and having come to know thousands of women between the ages of eighteen and twenty-six, her assessment that contemporary culture, is "toxic" to women carries considerable weight. "It is no coincidence," she goes on to say, "that the two top prescribed drugs at our state university's health center are anti-depressants and the birth control pill." Given the current situation, Professor Maloney is not at all surprised to observe that the number of women suffering from eating disorders, addiction, anxiety, and depression is at an all-time high.

It would be an understatement to say that these women are not enjoying their new freedom. But freedom that rejects virtue is really enslavement. Freedom from virtue is self-defeating no matter how appealing it may appear when it is marketed.

Saint John Paul II, writing as Karol Wojtyla, made the following statement in *Love & Responsibility*: "What is truly immodest in dress is that which frankly contributes to the deliberate displacement of the true value of the person by sexual values, that which is bound to elicit a reaction to the person as to a 'possible means of obtaining sexual enjoyment' and not 'a possible object of love by reason of his or her personal value.'" Simply stated, modesty is on the side of personality; immodesty is impersonal. Why would anyone prefer the impersonal to the personal, since we are, as a matter of fact, persons?

Modesty is a way of imperfectly concealing one's talents. Immodesty is more immediately conspicuous than modesty. That is because immodesty is superficial whereas modesty shuns the ostentatious. When Abraham

Lincoln stated that "The world will little note, nor long remember what we say here, but can never forget what they did here," his self-effacement was a fine example of modesty. And yet, his exceptional modesty did not conceal the splendor of his *Gettysburg Address*. In fact, it probably added to it. If ever a person rose to the occasion, it was America's sixteenth president on the battlefield of Gettysburg, Pennsylvania.

Modesty does not prevent a person's beauty, talent, or excellence from shining through. But it does allow these traits to become evident, slowly over time in the context of a personal relationship. Moreover, it allows such personal revelation to unfold without the distracting alloy of pride. Modesty opens the door to a relationship. Immodesty quickly burns itself out. Modesty is nourishment; immodesty is stimulation.

Hollywood is the world's capital of glamor, glitter, and glitz. Yet, these are not qualities that feed the soul. My modesty proposal, especially to young women, is for them to adopt this virtue that will not only be a source of empowerment for them, but of attractiveness in the best sense.

Venerable Carla Ronci

Time Tested Beauty Tips

For attractive lips, speak words of kindness.

For lovely eyes, seek out the good in people.

For a slim figure, share your food with the hungry.

For beautiful hair, let a child run his or her fingers
through it once a day.

For poise, walk with the knowledge that you never walk alone.

People, even more than things, have to be restored, renewed,
revived, reclaimed and redeemed; never throw out anyone.

Remember, if you ever need a helping hand, you'll find one
at the end of each of your arms.

As you grow older, you will discover that you have two hands,
one for helping yourself, the other for helping others.

The beauty of a woman is not in the clothes she wears,
the figure that she carries or the way she combs her hair.

The beauty of a woman must be seen from in her eyes, because
that is the doorway to her heart, the place where love resides.

The beauty of a woman is not in a facial mode but the true
beauty in a woman is reflected in her soul. It is the caring that
she lovingly gives the passion that she shows.

The beauty of a woman grows with the passing years.

Sam Levenson

AUDREY HEPBURN'S BEAUTY TIPS

The title of this article is misleading. It attributes a poem to the stylish actress that she did not compose. It happened to be one of her favorite poems and she read it to her children on the very last Christmas Eve she spent on earth. Legend credits her with its authorship. In her defense, she never claimed to have written it. The poem begins with the following advice that is patently more personal than cosmetic:

"For attractive lips, speak words of kindness. For lovely eyes, seek out the good in people. For a slim figure, share your food with the hungry. For beautiful hair, let a child run his or her fingers through it once a day. For poise, walk with the knowledge you'll never walk alone. People, even more than things, have to be restored, renewed, revived, reclaimed, and redeemed; Never throw out anybody."

The poem has been well received. The notion that one of Hollywood's most beautiful actresses saw fit to stress to her children the superiority of spiritual beauty over physical beauty is itself very beautiful. She was also admired for her courage. As a teenager, she was a carrier for the Belgian Underground Anti-Nazi movement during World War II. Popular sentiment wanted her to have written the poem. Nonetheless, Audrey Hepburn did not write what is popularly known as "Audrey Hepburn's Beauty Tips". It was originally composed by Sam Levenson and titled, "Time Tested Beauty Tips," which he wrote for his grandchild.

The last four words, for Sam Levenson, known to North Americans mostly as a comedian, were of special significance for him. In a short piece he wrote called "The Fate of the World," he stated his belief that "each newborn child arrives on earth with a message to deliver to mankind. Clenched in his little fist is some particle of yet unrevealed truth, some clue, which may solve the enigma of man's destiny."

India's Nobel Laureate, Rabindranath Tagore, said something similar when he commented that "Every child comes with the message that God is not yet discouraged of man." And in the same vein, Carl Sandburg, one of America's most celebrated poets, declared that "A baby is God's opinion that the world should go on." "Never will a time come," he went on to say, "when the most marvelous recent invention is as marvelous as a newborn child." A child is not an "inconvenience" nor is it "a consumer of valuable resources," as is commonly said to be the case. Sociologist George Gilder reports an instance when a woman sharply rebuked a man for fathering five children. "Don't you realize," she remonstrated, that they are "consumers of valuable natural resources"? The father replied, "But don't you realize that children are our most important natural resource!" Our concern for the environment has depreciated the value of new life. Yet, we are the custodians of the environment. The "garden" of Eden did not cultivate itself. Without humans there is no horticulture, agriculture or any other kind of culture.

Levenson is in good company concerning the value he places on the life of every newborn child. The child who comes into the world has a message. Correspondingly, we have an obligation to care for that child: "Our mission," he writes, "is to exercise the kind of loving care which will prompt the child to open his fist and offer up his truth, his individuality, the irreducible atom of his self." Faithful to his Jewish faith, Levenson stands by the philosophy expressed in Sanhedrin 4:4 which says that whoever destroys one life will be considered as having destroyed the whole world; and whoever saves one life will be credited with having saved the whole world.

ANXIETY AND PEACE

We all experience anxiety to one degree or another. St. Paul's words in Philippians 4:6-7 are as needed as they are consoling: "Dismiss all anxiety from your minds. Present your needs to God in every form of prayer and in petitions full of gratitude. Then God's own peace, which is beyond all understanding, will stand guard over your hearts and minds, in Christ Jesus."

It is encouraging to know that the anxiety we feel is not far from the peace we yearn. God is the Mediator who can exchange anxiety for that special form of peace that passes all understanding. But what is anxiety, a topic many modern existentialist philosophers have examined meticulously?

The German-American existentialist philosopher Paul Tillich, listed in the Pontifical Council for Culture's report on the New Age (f.n. 15) as one of the figures who had a great influence on the New Age Movement (along with Teilhard de Chardin, Carl Jung, Abraham Maslow, Carl Rogers, Aldous Huxley, and others) sees anxiety as the result of our acute awareness that our existence, in one way or another, is in peril. And it is in peril because we are finite, highly vulnerable beings who do not have complete control over the events of our life.

We try to do the best we can, and yet something happens, call it fate or bad luck, and our best laid plans are torn asunder. Therefore, as Tillich writes, "Non-being threatens man's self-affirmation." This is to say that the being we hope for can, at any moment, collapse into the non-being we dread.

Tillich's language is metaphysical. Nevertheless, it is easy enough to translate his language into something visual and readily accessible. Imagine the center fielder on a baseball team. The terrain he is obliged to cover is considerable. From a visual perspective, he seems to be just a speck in an ocean of space. There is far more room for the batted ball to land, than the ground he is able to cover. As he assumes his position prior to the game, with his cap held across his heart, he is an image of courage, a soldier, as it were, willing to accept his task in spite of being dwarfed by a sea of negative possibilities. He is willing to stand for being despite being surrounded by non-being. The same can be said for parents raising their children, or a writer trying to produce a novel. The room for failure seems to exceed the possibilities for success.

According to Tillich, there have been three different kinds of anxiety that have dominated three different ages in human history. In the ancient world, since life expectancy was short, anxiety about fate and death prevailed. In the medieval period, when faith was in flower, it was anxiety about guilt and condemnation that was dominant. The anxiety that characterizes the modern world is a sense of emptiness that leads to utter meaninglessness. The common denominator for all three of these anxieties is recognition of the possibility of personal dissolution. The fact that we experience anxiety is owed to our human condition which is frail, weak and vulnerable. We are not exactly masters of our domain, a truth about ourselves that we cannot completely suppress. Tillich refers to this condition as "existential anxiety." What this means is that we experience anxiety because of the nature of our existence. Therefore, this form of anxiety is perfectly normal.

But existential anxiety, though perfectly normal, can get the best of us if we do not do something about it. Tillich and other existential philosophers recommend courage, "the courage to be." Without this courage, they contend, what is normal can degenerate into something pathological. Normal anxiety can serve to motivate us. Abnormal anxiety can seriously interfere with our well-being. A person might have a certain anxiety about going to the dentist. A little bit of courage and a realization of the importance of good dental hygiene, however, can spur him on. On the other hand, without these motivational factors or others, he chooses not visit his dentist and must pay the consequence, thus falling from a better sense of being to an experience of non-being. This is why Tillich defines a neurosis as "a way of avoiding non-being by avoiding being." The musician is so terrified of making mistakes that he is unable to perform. The suitor is so fearful of being rejected that he decides not to propose. The job candidate is so anxious about failing the interview that he avoids it and stays home. These are counterproductive strategies.

The solution that Tillich and other existential thinkers offer, namely courage, is sound and helpful. Nonetheless, it is limited. It may lead to a sense of triumph, but it is not the sure road to peace. St. Paul is stressing the essential importance of prayer and uniting ourselves with Christ. We are finite; God is infinite. We are vulnerable; God is omnipotent. Courage can carry us only so far. Counselling, relaxation, and meditation are also helpful. Nonetheless, we need a remedy that does not possess the weaknesses that are inherent in our nature. We cannot pull ourselves up by our bootstraps. We must go outside of ourselves. God alone, therefore, can be the final solution for any anxiety that assails us.

The natural cannot be elevated by the mere natural. Existential philosophy, while helpful, cannot completely eradicate existential anxiety. Only the supernatural, the grace of God can bring about the peace to which St. Paul refers. Scripture reminds us that we should look to God to overcome the anxieties that mere existential remedies may leave behind: "When I am afraid, I will trust in you" (*Psalm* 56:3). "So do not fear, for I am with you; do not be dismayed, for I am your God. I will strengthen you and help you; I will uphold you with my righteous right hand" (*Isaiah* 41:10). "Cast all your anxieties upon Him because he cares for you" (*1 Peter* 5:7).

Vestibule by Kurelek

FOUR
ONE WAY

STOP AND GO, BUT DON'T THINK

It may very well be that my philosophical nature inclines me to value the Stop Sign above traffic lights. This may seem to be an odd and arbitrary preference, but there are good reasons for it, especially if one thinks symbolically. The latter represents a mechanical stop-and-go instruction that reminds me too much of our mechanized way of life. We are busy creatures and become anxious when we are required to pause for the red light to change to green. It is symbolic of a hurried life style, but also of one in which we are told what our next step will be. We find ourselves marching to a mechanized beat.

The Stop Sign, on the other hand, tells us only to "stop," while gently allowing us to determine when we should move on. It respects our freedom and initiative while safeguarding us from oncoming traffic. It allows us to think. It gives us pause, not in the manner in which Coca Cola offers us the pause that refreshes, but as the opportunity to look around and see what we might have otherwise missed.

There is considerable wisdom in the popular maxim "Stop and smell the roses." A recent study done at Rutgers University, and reported in the *Journal of Personality and Individual Differences*, indicates that taking the time to appreciate people and the little things in life can play in important role in our overall happiness. Even taking the time, literally, to smell flowers, can be a healthy antidote to what is called the "rat race" in which we often find ourselves.

Jean-Pierre de Caussade, of the Society of Jesus, wrote *The Sacrament of the Present Moment* to help his readers hear God's voice as He speaks to us at every moment, and with love. This 300-year-old classic asks us to put aside our ego and pride so that we can be open to God's salvific grace that is available from moment to moment. Each day, the author assures us, is a sacrament that we should not ignore.

In another 300-year-old classic, *The Practice of the Presence of God*, Brother Lawrence advises us that "whatever we do, even if we are reading the Word or praying, we should stop for a few minutes—as often as possible—to praise God from the depths of our hearts, to enjoy Him there in secret." "Why shouldn't you stop," he asks, "for a while to adore Him, to petition Him, to offer Him your heart, and to thank Him?" There should be many stop signs in our daily lives that invite us to listen to the voice of God. The horizontal dimension of life should not eclipse our vertical relationship with the transcendent.

"The world is too much with us; late and soon," said the poet, William Wordsworth: "Getting and spending, we lay waste our powers; little we see in Nature that is ours; we have given our hearts away, a sordid boon." Our excessive preoccupation with money has dulled our spiritual faculties. We have traded in *Homo Sapiens* for *Homo Economicus*. There is little time to stop and think. Our lives remain unexamined; our destiny, undiscovered. Speed robs us of the opportunity to appreciate all the beauty that lies around us.

Speed has become a central characteristic of our culture. The 1982 movie, *Fast Times at Ridgemont High*, is an excellent encapsulation of America's love affair with speed. It portrays teenagers trying to grow up too fast, working at fast-food restaurants, engaging in fast sex, listening to fast music, and taking fast-acting drugs. There is no time either to think or to live. Unfortunately the movie was regarded more for its entertainment value than for its timely moral message.

Technology, from speedways to the high speed Internet, has certainly sped up our lives, but at the price of reducing our face-to-face relationships and opportunities to appreciate the sacrament of the moment. In walking to work, we become involved in a host of interpersonal exchanges. If we ride a bicycle, these exchanges are fewer. But if we take the car, though we gain in speed, we lose in personal encounters. Getting there becomes all-important. A character by the name of Yonatan Frimer has recited Hamlet's "To Be or Not To Be' Soliloquy in less than a minute. At this speed, however, the message is completely unintelligible. It is fair to say that Shakespeare would have preferred a slower pace. Speed obscures. In "getting there" faster, speed erases all the vital experiences we could have enjoyed along the way. Life is to be lived, not rushed.

Mozart, who knew something about music, taught that the silent moments between the notes were more important than the notes themselves. This is a key to understanding the spiritual significance of his music. We might also say that in those silent moments between one action and another we begin to appreciate and enjoy the life that surrounds us, and perhaps even hear the Word of God. We need to stop and think, rather than stop and go. We need to meditate, to look over what we often overlook, to count our blessings. Life should not be a high-speed, endless merry-go-round, but the continuing opportunity to savor the blessings that God has strewn at our feet.

THE SECRET OF LONGEVITY

The Sequoia tree *(Sequoiadendron giganteum)* is the largest living thing on the planet. The oldest living sequoia is estimated to be 2,200 years although there is scientific evidence, through carbon dating, that this extraordinary plant can remain alive as long 3,200 years. "General Sherman," the name given to the largest living example of the species, is located in northern California's Sequoia National Park. It is more than 275 feet high, has a base diameter of 102 feet, and contains approximately 52,508 cubic feet of wood.

Given their massive surface area, one would expect that high winds could easily cause them to topple over. Such is not the case, however. Sequoias typically live in groves, within a community, so to speak, of other Sequoias. Although their roots penetrate only between 6 to 20 feet below the ground, something rather fortuitous takes place that allows them to remain standing even during severe windstorms. The secret to their longevity lies in the fact that their roots spread across a wide area and intertwine with the roots of other Sequoias. As mighty as this tree appears above the ground, it owes its longevity to a sub-visible community of roots that bind themselves together. They are, quite literally "well-grounded". "United they stand; divided they would fall." "President Lincoln" might have been a more suitable name for the largest of the living Sequoias.

An analogy between the Sequoia tree and the human person is irresistible. We find an analogy between tree and man in *Deuteronomy* 20:19-20: "When you besiege a city a long time, to make war against it in order to capture it, you shall not destroy its trees by swinging an axe against them; for you may feast from them, and you shall not cut them down. For is the tree of the field a man, that it should be besieged by you?" The special value of trees is underscored in *Isaiah* 60:13: "The glory of Lebanon will come to you, the juniper, the box tree and the cypress together, to beautify the place of My sanctuary; and I shall make the place of My feet glorious." Did Daniel have a vision of a Sequoia tree when he said, "Thus [were] the visions of mine head in my bed; I saw, and behold a tree in the midst of the earth, and the height thereof [was] great" (*Daniel* 4:10-12).

We find numerable references to trees throughout Scripture: the tree in the Garden of Eden, the tree of Jesse, the fig tree, the tree of life with its twelve kinds of fruit, poplar, almond, olive, and plane trees, and David's musical instrument made of fir wood.

The mighty Sequoia can be used to symbolize the person. Whereas the Sequoia owes its longevity to its sub-visible roots; man owes his longevity to roots that are invisible. God sustains us. But, in addition, we survive, prosper, and thrive thanks to the invisible cords that bind us in our friendships with others. As mere individuals, no matter how tall we stand, we are vulnerable. As the poet Lord Byron put it, "Happiness was born a twin". It is an old story. Isolation from others breeds misery. As the sixteenth century philosopher, Lao Tze sadly remarked, "Though neighboring communities overlook one another and the crowing of cocks and barking of dogs can be heard, yet the people there may grow old and die without ever visiting each other."

The Sequoia tree reminds us that we are persons, which is to say, that we are both visible individuals and, at the same time, bound to each other by invisible ties. This stupendous example of plant life refutes the individualism that has so haunted the modern world since Rene Descartes (I think, therefore I am, but I am not so sure about you) and the ideology of Karl Marx which contends that man is merely a part of the collective."

Jacques Maritain is severe in his denunciation of both radical individualism and atheistic communism. His critique of the former, however, may resonate better with the individualism of North American society. In his *Three Reformers*, he states that "the modern city sacrifices the person to the individual [giving] equal rights, liberty of opinion, to the individual, and delivers the person, isolated, naked, with no social framework to support and protect it, to all the devouring powers that threaten the soul's life." It is as if society is saying to the vulnerable individual: "You are a free individual. Defend yourself, save yourself, all by yourself." And this is why Maritain sees fit to describe the naked individualism of the modern world as constituting a "homicidal civilization". In *Without Roots* (2006), co-authored by Joseph Ratzinger and the atheist philosopher, Marcello Pera, the latter makes the comment that "The only thing worse than living without roots is struggling to get by without a future". If we are not well-grounded, can we survive?

Saint Paul VI used the image of the tree to describe the way in which the Church has developed. "This is how the Lord wanted his church to be," he wrote, "universal, a great tree whose branches shelter the birds of the air . . . In the mind of the Lord the Church is universal by vocation and mission, but when she puts her roots in a variety of social and human terrains, she takes on different external expressions and appearances in each part of the world" (*Exarchat Apostoloque*, 1992).

Our roots must be placed in the invisible, but providential protection of God, without forgetting our rootedness in love, friendship, and civility. Here, like that of the Church, is the secret to our longevity.

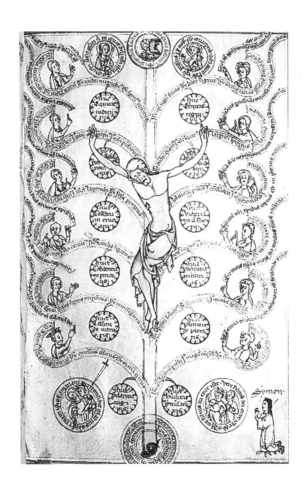

HOW TO PUT THEM ON

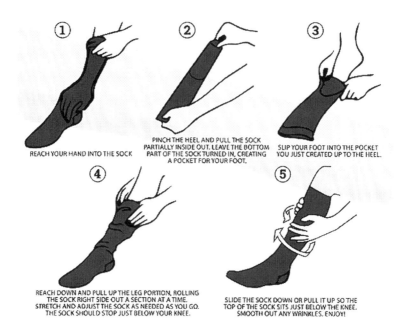

PHILOSOPHY'S PRACTICALITY

Bill Maher, who is not my favorite comedian, has said that philosophy is about as useful as a bidet in a gorilla cage. Well, a bidet may be of no use to a gorilla, but philosophy is certainly of great use to us human beings. As a matter of fact, we could not begin to get dressed in the morning without drawing upon a constellation of philosophical principles. We depend on philosophy far more than we realize. Philosophy, in fact, is so basic that it is usually employed without our noticing its abiding presence. It was not until 1774 that oxygen was discovered. Yet, despite this relatively recent discovery by Joseph Priestly, people had never refrained from breathing in this life-sustaining, though invisible, gas. Our knowledge of things often comes long after we have derived their benefits. Getting dressed in the morning is an example of this paradoxical phenomenon.

The alarm clock sounds and we rise. We are, after all, bipeds and belong to the biological classification of *Homo erectus*. We are not dormitive creatures, since that term does not capture our full nature. Sleep is for restoration; it is not our destination. We are rational beings and begin the task of getting dressed utilizing that essential quality by which we are distinguished from brute animals. Thus we begin our day by putting philosophy into practice. We put our socks on before we slip into our shoes. The reverse would be "preposterous". This word must have been coined by a philosopher since it warns us against the disorder that occurs when we put "before" (*pre-*) what should be "posterior" (*posterius*). We must open our mouths before we brush our teeth. You must catch the ball before you tag the runner. Lincoln was a rail splitter before he became president. And so, by avoiding the preposterous, our day begins in an orderly way.

We notice that our socks are not only equal but identical. We might say, "that's the way it is". In Spanish, the previous sentence reads: *esso si que es*, fortuitously sounding out S O C K S. There is no left or right sock. But our shoes, though equally shoes, are not identical. They are complementary, one belonging to the left foot, the other to its complementary opposite. On reflection, we may also recognize that socks and shoes both belong to the genus of clothing. Hence, we are also logicians. We encounter no difficulty or hesitation in donning our shoes and socks, unmindful of the fact that this simple activity assumes our acceptance of rationality, order, equality, identity, complementarity, and logic. We are all philosophers at the break of day. But during the day we often fail to employ the philosophical values that we affirmed in our mundane task of putting on our socks and shoes.

Saint John XXIII remarked that the sexes are equal in humanity but complementary in mission. The reigning liberal position now is that the sexes are not complementary but only seem so because of cultural conditioning. Yet nature does precede culture, a stubborn fact that seems to be overlooked in the current world. When we become too thoughtful about anything, we often lose sight of what it really is. According to the fable, the millipede is paralyzed when it tries to figure out which of its thousand legs it should move first and in what sequence. Analysis can provoke paralysis. Robert Bork has made the comment that the major obstacles to religious belief in the contemporary world are provided by members of the intellectual class who contend that "science has left atheism as the only respectable intellectual stance." It might be worth stating that there would be no science if there were no created world. Nor would there be any atheists if there were no God. Creation precedes our understanding of it.

When asked the secret of his success, famed novelist Somerset Maugham once said that it was because each day he did two things he was reluctant to do: "go to bed at night and get up in the morning". Implicit in his remark is reason's victory over inertia and an affirmation that one has a better chance of achieving success when he accords priority to reason over self-indulgence. It is also an affirmation that we are rational by nature, a point that has found agreement among the great philosophers of history. Allowing our emotions to displace reason is another example of being "preposterous," or, to put it into the context of the history of philosophy, it exemplifies putting Descartes before "des-horse". Descartes' mistake was putting *thinking* ("I think therefore I am") ahead of being (I am first and foremost a human being). And this is why he is dubbed The Father of Modern Confusion. One has to be a human being first before he can engage in thinking.

194

Etienne Gilson has pointed out that a terrible thing happens when we put man first and God second. The consequence of this preposterous arrangement is that God disappears. Atheism is the inevitable result. God, of course, cannot remain God if He is demoted. In this case He is lost and his rediscovery becomes exceedingly difficult. Atheism may be grounded more in an exaggerated belief in man than in a denial of God.

In *Troilus and Cressida*, Shakespeare has Ulysses ask how we can obtain honey when the general is not distinguished from the hive. "The heavens themselves," Ulysses tells his troops, "the planets and this centre observe degree, priority and place." Things must "stand in authentic place," he declares. "Take but degree away, untune that string, and, hark, what discord follows! Each thing meets in mere oppugnancy." Wise Ulysses understands that on the battlefield, disorder, another name for the preposterous, breeds defeat.

When we slow down the process of such an everyday routine as getting dressed and put our mind to the underlying principles behind what we are doing, we can rediscover the practicality of philosophy. In a sense, philosophy is like oxygen, something that is necessary but unseen. We may begin the day on the right foot, so to speak, and then enter a world where discord reigns. It is a world in which the human unborn are denied their human nature, where money takes precedence over morality, and God is denied His authentic place.

Edna St. Vincent Millay

Phyllis McGinley

THE ROLE OF THE HEART IN CATHOLIC EDUCATION

I was watching the telecast of a baseball game between the Minnesota Twins and the New York Yankees. The Twins first baseman, Joe Mauer was at the plate. The pitch count ran to 3 and 2 whereupon the unrelenting batter continued to foul off pitch after pitch. When the 13th pitch was about to be delivered, the broadcaster informed his audience that this is the greatest number of pitches ever thrown to Joe Mauer in a single at bat. During his fourteen year career with the Twins, he has had 7417 plate appearances. I was amazed that this bit of information, which scanned a prodigious mass of data, could be retrieved so quickly. But this is the modern world of useless and trivial data: technological wizardry at the service of providing mind-numbingly unimportant information.

The American poet, Edna St. Vincent Millay, who won the Pulitzer Prize for *Poetry* in 1923, was concerned about this problem of spinning out useless information and expressed it poetically:

> Upon this gifted age, in its dark hour,
> Rains from the sky a meteoric shower
> Of facts . . . they lie unquestioned, uncombined
> Wisdom enough to leech us of our ill
> Is daily spun, but there exists no loom
> To weave it into fabric.

In retrospect, her observation was as perceptive as it was prophetic. Alongside the shower of information is the drought of wisdom. The "loom" to which she refers is no doubt the heart, for it is the heart that combines, unifies, integrates, and gives meaning to things. America's most distinguished educator, Mortimer Adler coined the term "alphabetiasis" to refer to the intellectual defect of arranging things alphabetically, but going no further. According the Adler, this malaise is a fairly recent one and is far more widespread than ever before in history. From the standpoint of education, obtaining or receiving information is only getting to first base. Information should lead to acquiring knowledge, supplementing knowledge with understanding and then reaching for wisdom.

We do not need schooling in order to obtain information. Facts and figures, data of endless variety are readily available from the computer. But the superhighway of information does not accommodate the needs of the heart. Literature, on the other hand, what Ezra Pound referred to as "news that stays news," engages not only the mind but the heart as well. And yet, literature has been replaced these days to some extent by the likes of "Shakespeare for Dummies". Pascal spoke of the heart and how it functions in an intuitive and integrative way ("*Le coeur a ses raison que la raison ne connaît point* — The heart has reasons that reason knows nothing of.) Surely, mathematician Bertrand Russell was not enlisting his heart when he said that if there is a god, it is a differential equation.

The gap between the mind and the heart did not escape the attention of Saint John Paul II. In his September 29, 1996 Angelus Address, he made the following comment: "Today's prevailing scientific culture puts an enormous quantity of information at our disposal; but every day it is apparent that this is not enough for an authentic process of humanization. We have greater need than ever to rediscover the dimensions of the 'heart'; we need more heart.

The former Pontiff devoted more extensive attention to the problem in his encyclical on Catholic education, *Ex Corde Ecclesiae*. It is instructive to note that the title's English translation reads, "Born from the Heart of the Church." The words "born," "heart," and "Church" (*ecclesia*) all have a maternal implication. If there is to be a renaissance in Catholic education, for Saint John Paul, it must incorporate these feminine elements. Again, it pertains to the feminine to give birth, to see things with the heart, and to embrace everyone in accordance with the mission of the Church. Phyllis McGinley's book, *The Province of the Heart* (1956) is a tribute to the unique sensibility that the woman brings to the world, a sensibility without which, everything would collapse into meaningless assemblage of facts.

Reality is an integrated phenomenon. Hence the appropriateness of the word "universe" which refers to one unified world. The Greek word "*kosmos*" referred to a universe that was not only, one, unified, and ordered, but beautiful as well. Scientists may take the world apart in order to better understand it, but they need, in the final analysis, to reintegrate it. It was the genius of Newton to see that force equaled the product of mass and acceleration. And it was the genius of Einstein to see that energy equalled the product of mass and the square of the speed of light. Reality cannot be decomposed and left scattered. Deconstruction is a philosophy that is essentially unfaithful to the order and unity of reality. Jacques Maritain's personal motto as a realistic philosopher was "Distinguish to Unite".

Ex Corde Ecclesiae was well received in Spain, Latin America, France, and Italy. The most negative reaction to it came from the United States where the notions of autonomy and academic freedom were more entrenched. The role of the heart in unifying things did not seem to be as important for American academics as going their own way. Nonetheless, in rejecting the spirit of the encyclical, Catholic education in the United States became more heavily influenced by secular thinking. The debate concerning the Catholic identity of Catholic colleges continued throughout Pope John's pontificate. Nonetheless, the integration of academic freedom with truth should be the aim of any serious educational institution.

Edna St. Vincent Millay was unduly pessimistic when she said, "there exists no loom". The loom is the heart, which is personified by the woman. John Paul II had this in mind in his 1995 *Letter To Women* where he referred to their natural integrative capacities: "Thank you, every woman, for the simple fact of being a woman! Through the insight which is so much a part of your womanhood you enrich the world's understanding and help to make human relationships more honest and authentic." That "insight" is rooted in the heart which is urgently needed in today's world of education.

PLAY IT AGAIN, SAM

Movie buffs know all too well that the words, "Play it again, Sam," were never uttered in the film, *Casablanca*. Ilsa, played by Ingrid Bergman, did say the piano player, (Dooley Wilson) "Play it," but did not articulate the word "again". Sam, however, did play the haunting song, *As Time Goes By*, again and again. Posterity has more than made up for that missing word. Woody Allen's 1972 movie, *Play It Again, Sam* was based on his 1969 Broadway play by the same title. There is an international record label know as  "Play it again, Sam Records." That persistent phrase also titles a 1989 work for solo viola by Milton Babbitt. It is a song and a branding used by Superior Software. The list goes on. The question: why is it that the missing word in Casablanca has been re-inserted so many times and remains one of the most notable misquotations in all of filmdom?

The answer is fairly simple. Whenever we experience something good, we want to experience it again. We are not content to hear a beautiful song just once. We want to hear it again and again. A dozen roses is a far better gift than a single rose. It would be a far poorer world if no rose ever repeated itself. We return to our favorite restaurant, celebrate anniversaries, and welcome the New Year. We love the repetition of everything we love.

The solar system is a symphony of repetition: the diurnal rotation of the earth on its axis, its annual rotation around the sun, the regularity of the lunar month, the alternation of the seasons, the planetary orbits. These repetitions conspire to produce cosmic harmony, unity and balance. On the atomic level, a similar symphony is played out involving the periodicity of electrons orbiting around their nuclei. The replication of the DNA molecule and mitotic division are the elementary activities required for organic reproduction. Repetition permeates the universe on every level.

Beethoven's Fifth Symphony, one of the most celebrated of all orchestral compositions, begins with a four note figure which is the thread, repeated in sundry ways, that weaves the first movement into a dramatic unity. It never lapses into anything akin to boredom or monotony, but remains invigorating and captivating. Repetition here is an expression of vitality. In the right hands, repetition becomes excitement without dullness, intensity without predictability. On a theological level, the Mass and the liturgical calendar attest to the importance of repetition.

The 1939 song, "We'll Meet Again," was one of the most endearing of the Second World War Era. It resonated powerfully with soldiers going off to war and the intense desire that family members and friends had for seeing them again: "We'll meet again, don't know where, don't know when. But I know we'll meet again some sunny day." The lyrics are nearly heartbreaking.

Bishop Fulton J. Sheen once stated that he could easily imagine God, with the exuberance of a child, saying every morning to the sun, "Do it again," and every evening saying to the moon and stars, "Do it again," and every springtime saying to the daisies, "Do it again," and every winter saying to the snowflakes, "Do it Again,". He welcomed every new child born into the world as a divine encore. God repeats Himself, so to speak, in a limitless number of ways because it is his nature to give. His richness overflows in an endless cascade of creativity. In fact, it is the very nature of being to give of itself. For St. Thomas Aquinas, the good diffuses itself (*Bonum est difussivum sui*). Therefore, it is because God is good that we exist. The Angelic Doctor also states that "it pertain to the notion of the good to communicate itself to others".

Plato recognized the innate inclination for repetition that exists in human beings. Accordingly, he wrote, "Happiness expresses itself in the desire to reproduce the beautiful." It is quite natural, therefore, for husband and wife to reproduce, just as it is natural for an artist to continue reproducing artifacts. The single experience never exhausts the plenitude of being. Love, joy, friendship, beauty all desire continual repetition. Once is never enough for the creative appetite. "He who would win joy must share it," wrote Lord Byron, "for happiness was born a twin."

If, in the contemporary world, enthusiasm for procreation has waned, it may very well be that it is because happiness, the engine of creativity, has also waned. To be happy is to be in touch with one's being. And it belongs to the nature of being to reproduce itself in some way. The happy person does not desire either isolation or sterility.

The first book of the Bible is *Genesis*, which is about generation. Generation, creation, reproduction, repetition, echo, and encore all attest to the built-in tendency of both God and man to "do it again". This tendency is most evident in children. Whenever they come upon something they enjoy, they want to do it again, and again. They love hearing the same story, listening to the same song, seeing the same trick, over and over again. Because the child is full of life, his appetite for fun is not satisfied by a single serving.

Christ said to Nicodemus that unless a man be born again, he cannot enter the Kingdom of God (John 3: 3). We cannot be content with the earthly life we have been given. We need to be reborn in the spirit. We must be sensitive to that spiritual dynamic within ourselves that urges us to higher things. We are born, but must be reborn to share more fully in God's life. Complacency is not the way of the Christian.

Casablanca has been repeated and re-appreciated numberless times by countless movie buffs over the past 70 years. So, too, has Sam played *As Time Goes By* for his cinematic viewers again and again. Time has corrected what Hollywood had omitted. We should welcome the repetitions in our life that give it energy and order.

John & Peter running to the tomb.

FIVE
RESUME SPEED

 # PROVIDENCE

The motto of Colorado is *Nil Nisi Numine*, which is translated as "Nothing without Providence". One might think that such a motto is more suitable for Rhode Island, for, without its State Capital, it is, in terms of land mass, virtually nothing. Nonetheless, the city of Providence, Rhode Island is not without a connection with Divine Providence. Roger Williams, a religious exile from the Massachusetts Bay Colony named the area in honor of "God's merciful Providence". He believed God had led him to discover such a fine haven for him and his followers to settle. Today, the city of Providence is home to eight hospitals and seven institutions of higher learning. Roger Williams may have had a point.

In the secular world, however, the word "providence" is more often associated with insurance companies and health plans than with God. One is being provident, it is said, by preparing for the future. In a well-known Aesop fable, the author illustrates that "It is best to prepare for the days of necessity" by comparing the grasshopper, who lives for the moment, and the provident ant, who prepares for tomorrow. In this regard, being provident is a virtue. Similarly, philosophers of antiquity viewed providence as simply an act of prudence. The question naturally arises, "Do we need God to prepare for the future"? After all, are we not in good hands with Allstate?

Saint Thomas Aquinas' discussion of Providence is especially helpful and instructive. He understands God's Providence in a twofold manner. First, God manifests his Providence in creation. In this way, God's demonstrates his Providence with regards to the "substance" of things (*Summa Theologica* I, 22, 1). But God would have abandoned his creatures if he left them to their mere existence. Therefore, He shows his Providential Care for his human creatures by endowing them with an inclination toward their end. Their end is also twofold including the particular end which is their natural good, and their supernatural end which is to be with God.

The word "providence" means to see things before they happen (*Pro* +

videre). Therefore, Aquinas states "It is necessary that the type of the order of things towards their end should pre-exist in the divine mind: and the type of things ordered towards an end is, properly speaking, providence." As a providential God, He gives us both our life and our direction. He sees what is good for us long before they come into being so that we can see them ourselves. His Providence does not preclude our freedom, for it is up to us to choose freely what is good for us. It must also be stated that, for Aquinas, God's Providence can be found in the particulars of a person's life. "For instance," as he writes, "the meeting of two servants, although to them it appears a chance circumstance, has been fully foreseen by their master, who has purposely sent them to meet at the one place, in such a way that the one knows not about the other" (*S.T.* I, 22, 2). In other words, we can sense the actions of divine Providence in the particular events and incidents of our daily lives. We are travelers. God gives us our life, our destination, and the provisions we need to reach our destination.

The debate between providence and chance is one that is as old as philosophy. The more we know, however, especially what science teaches us, the more the notion that we are guided by a Divine Agent becomes irrefutable. Consider the development of human life from the initial zygote stage.

Although it is no larger than a grain of sugar, the single-cell zygote contains a complete genetic code, all the DNA and all the genes that a complete human being will ever need. This tiny zygote initiates a development that progresses to form the 30-trillion cell adult. At the same time, it exerts biochemical and hormonal influences on the mother as it begins to control and direct the process of pregnancy, a power amplification, considering its miniscule size in relation to that of the mother, that is utterly astonishing. Moreover, it impresses itself, through its DNA, on all the generations of its descendants just as all the generations of its ancestors have impressed their own genotype on it. Accordingly, world-class geneticist Jérôme Lejeune states in his book, *The Concentration Can*, "As no other information will enter later into the zygote, the fertilized egg, one is forced to admit that all the necessary and sufficient information to define that particular creature is found together at fertilization."

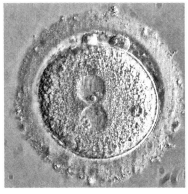

How could it be possible for a single cell to develop on its own to a perfectly integrated human organism of 30 trillion cells by chance? Moreover, the infant human produces 200 neurons in his brain per minute. This prodigious rate actually slows down a bit in the adult brain and settles in to form a brain of roughly 100 billion neurons. A large hotel, given all its wiring, plumbing, heating ducts, and everything else that goes into it, is not nearly as complex as the cellular complexity of but one of its guests. Furthermore, a similarly organized complexity exists for all plants and animals.

Aquinas is fully in agreement with the *Book of Wisdom* and cites the following passage with approval: "She reaches from end to end mightily, and orders all things sweetly" (Wisdom 8:1).

From Kurelek's Passion of Christ

THE REALISM OF CHRISTIANITY

The prevailing assumption in the secular world is that science is a reliable pathway to reality whereas religion, although a source of hope for many, is fundamentally unrealistic. A strong case, however, can be made that science is largely theoretical and cannot provide a basis for authentic living, while religion, particularly Christianity, is not only eminently practical, but far more realistic than science. The following ten points serve to make the case for the realism of Christianity.

First, the realism of man:

What is a human being? What is man that God is mindful of him? He is not simply an individual, according to the Cartesian tradition, nor is he merely a member of the collective, according to the ideology of the Marxists. The concept of the human being in the secular world oscillates between man as a mere individual who has rights but few duties, and man as a member of society who has many duties but few rights.

Christian philosophers, including Jacques Maritain, Nikolai Berdyaev, and St. John Paul II, have been at pains to explain that a human being is, in reality, a person, that is, a dynamic integration of unique individuality and communal responsibility. He is called to love, and in love finds his truest self.

Second, the realism of sex:

God created them male and female. A person's sex is the first thing we notice in another and the last thing we are likely to forget. Its identity is marked in each of the several trillion cells that constitute the body of the human being. It is not fluid, changing from one to the other. Nor is it merely a convention. In reality, male and female are complementary.

Neither sex is self-sufficient. As complementary opposites, male and female assist each other in becoming whole, psychologically, morally, and personally.

Third, the realism of marriage:

The realism of marriage follows the nature of the human being as a sexual person who has the capacity to become a two-in-one-flesh partner with another. The unity of man and woman in marriage also includes the natural capacity for procreation. Marriage is a most exceptional form of friendship because of its profound unity and the pledge of fidelity that honors its particular value.

Statistically, married people live longer and are more strongly motivated than their unmarried counterparts, a strong indication of the realism of marriage.

Fourth, the realism of the family:

The family is the basic unit of society and bears upon the health of society's future. "The future of mankind passes through the family," as St. John Paul II was fond of saying. The family is the fruitful achievement of a man and a woman living together in a bond of love that produces offspring who are themselves loved, cared for, and educated. Children bless marriage. Grandchildren are their grandparents' "crown," as Scripture claims.

Fifth, the realism of altruism:

At the heart of Christianity is the mandate to love one's neighbor. If this mandate were to be carried out, peace would reign and war would be relegated to the vault of history. The neighbor is "another self." The relationship between one person and another, then, takes on the form of "I-Thou." Expressing love toward one's neighbor is the only realistic solution in working toward ending poverty and overcoming the loneliness that afflicts untold millions of human beings.

Sixth, the realism of society:

The fact that the realism of the family is the basic unit of society logically leads to Christianity's understanding of the realism of society. One realism prepares the way for another. According to the tenets of Christianity, the factors that make for a good society are not wealth, status, and power, but virtue, neighborliness, and love. One of the essential responsibilities of parents is to educate and prepare their children for their productive role in society.

Seventh, the realism of religion:

It is not the function of religion to wallow in superstition, but to locate basic truths that science cannot provide. Christianity reveals truths about man, God, and the afterlife that have their foundation in a realistic philosophy, and add to it. Given the finite abilities of the human being, it is reasonable to conclude that he needs help from above. Moreover, this help for Christians is also provided in the form of sacraments. Man needs God. Without God, as history has shown, man sets himself against man.

Eight, the realism of life:

Life is a gift. It is all we have. Without this gift we would never have existed. Therefore, life must be received with gratitude and regarded as our most cherished possession. The Christian, therefore, finds it easy to believe that working for a Culture of Life is far more reasonable and realistic than allowing a Culture of Death to prevail. He values human life in all its forms and at all its stages.

Ninth, the realism of death:

The denial of death is a common feature in a secular world that does not believe in an afterlife. Nothing is more unrealistic, however, than to deny that which is inevitable. The Christian, with St. Paul, agrees than death has neither "sting" nor "victory." Death is a passage to another world. An endless life under earthly conditions, ever growing older and ever becoming more feeble, would mean that life ultimately has no meaning. It is death that gives life meaning.

Tenth, the realism of God:

God is the ultimate reality. He is the source of everything that is. We know that nothing we observe has the intrinsic power to generate itself. Everything we know comes from something prior to it. God is the great Beginning. He creates and governs the universe and everything the universe contains. He is the light that illuminates what little we know. He holds the answers to all the mysteries that now perplex our minds. He is the final piece of the puzzle that completes all things and gives them their ultimate meaning.

Christianity is hardly a fiction. It is intensely realistic. In fact, its realism is the primary reason that it has outlasted all other institutions over the past two millennia. Christianity is realistic. But its realism is not overpowering. Although it appeals to the intellect, its membership requires an act of the will. A person must choose to be a Christian.

THE IMPORTANCE OF HOLIDAYS

Bishop Fulton J. Sheen fully appreciated the value of humor. He would invariably open his TV show, *Life Is Worth Living*, which was watched back in the 1950's by an audience estimated to be in the neighborhood of thirty million viewers, with a joke or a funny story. He knew that humor was double-edged. It could make a point as well as make people laugh, appealing both to the mind and to the funny bone. One of my favorite of his one-liners is his reference to the man who was an atheist for a year, but had to give it up because there were no holidays.

Sheen's witticism actually complements atheists for it implies that they have a sense of the holy and long for it when it is missing from their lives. Dana Gioia, California's reigning poet laureate agrees with Sheen in principle, and credits the Church for being a kind of specialist when it comes to cultivating a sense of the holy. "What Catholicism does is inform my work," he states, "Whether the poem is about an angel or an alley way, my way of seeing the world (and sensing what lies beyond the visible world) is always Catholic." He cites Psalm 96 which instructs us to "Worship the Lord in the splendor of his holiness" and adds, "A nonbeliever should be able to feel the truth and majesty of the Church."

No doubt, because Sheen was a philosopher, he believed that the "point" of his humor was more important than the laugh it might evoke. And the "point" was usually a way of making his moral message irresistible. His artful humor brings to mind the words of the esteemed 18th century essayist Joseph Addison: "I shall endeavor to enliven morality with wit and temper wit with morality." The humorist must depict morality as attractive and take care not to make it appear unseemly.

A holiday, as the word implies, is a "holy day". Holiness is not derived from the earth. Its origin is from on high. Christmas is our most popular holiday because it offers something that the world cannot provide: peace, brotherhood, and enduring love. A life without holidays is a life immersed in a world that cannot fulfill our deepest desires. Such a life renders a person a cosmic orphan, reducing him to just another meaningless atom within an infinite sea of other meaningless atoms.

Although holiness originates from on high, its reality is readily accessible. The world is diaphanous. It allows us to see through it so that we have glimpses, hints, or intimations of the holy. Life would be unbearably barren without any sense whatsoever of the holy. Christmas celebrates the arrival of the Most Holy, the One who penetrates our hearts and sanctifies our souls. It gives us a booster shot of what we are able to sense, perhaps more dimly, on a daily basis. As C. S. Lewis states in *Miracles*, "The Supernatural is not remote and abstruse: it is a matter of daily and hourly experience, as intimate as breathing."

For Saint Thomas Aquinas, the Natural Law participates in the Eternal Law. It is a doorway, so to speak, into a realm that is richer and purer than the one in which we live. Thus, for the Angelic Doctor, everything has a "certain hidden secret) or a "sacred secret" [*(sacrum secretum) Summa Theologica* III, 60, 1]. All things contain God's secret signature.

Shakespeare added a touch of poetry to this insight in *As You Like It* where, walking through the Forest of Arden, one "Finds tongues in trees, books in running brooks, sermons in stones, and good in everything." Yet, for the perspicacious, this enchanted forest encompasses the entire globe. Accordingly, for C. S. Lewis, we discover "patches of God-light in the woods of our experience". This "light" assures us that there is more to reality than meets the eye. We are not bound by the lower order of things. The eternal flashes before our mind. The epitaph that Cardinal Newman chose for himself was "Coming out from the shadows into Reality" (*ex umbris et imaginibus in veritatem*).

Alfred Lord Tennyson's little poem, *Flower in the Crannied Wall,* is large in implication, bringing the finite and the infinite into contact with each other. Holding the flower in his hands the poet states that "if I could understand what you are, root and all, and all in all, I should know what God and man is." The word "if" offers the possibility of sensing the divine in the ephemeral. Our lives are an unceasing attempt to translate the "if" into a realization.

Out of the Depths by Kurelek

It is easy for us to imagine Sheen's atheist as being smitten by metaphysical claustrophobia. Being so constricted, boredom becomes inevitable. The attempt to escape from boredom is a national pastime. But immersing oneself even more in things that are not holy, drugging ourselves with shopping, eating, and drinking, fails to solve the problem. The key that unlocks our prison house is the sense of the holy that surrounds us. And the passages to escape are virtually everywhere. The Christmas Season offers us a splendid opportunity to revel in the glory of a holiday so that our vision is enlarged, having been liberated from a closed and calculating world. Christmas is God's personal response to the temptation to atheism.

Ukrainian Christmas Eve by Kurelek

CHRISTMAS

Christmas is about birth and rebirth. It is about the birth of our Savior and our own rebirth. It is the great antidote to life that is hurdling toward death. Poetry is also about birth and rebirth. In its own humble way, it, too, is an argument against death being the final chapter of our lives. Virgil, the greatest of the Latin poets, said that "There are tears in things, and all things that are doomed to die touch the heart" (*Lachrimae rerum; et mentem mortalia tangunt*). But he did not know about Christmas and how the birth of the Christ-child means the victory of light over darkness, love over hate, and life over death. Christmas brings back to life so many fond memories of friends we have almost forgotten. Mortality continues to elicit tears, but Christmas, that transcends our finitude, is the great harbinger of unfettered joy and lasting life.

The birth of Christ stirs our memories that may have been

Dormant, like a child's slumber, for nearly a dozen months,

Occasioning a second birth to a myriad of friends our hearts hold dear,

Evoking pleasant times, bright smiles, warm hugs,
and joy-filled conversations.

Our memories, like swaddling clothes, wrap you with our affection
as we await,

Like shepherds in the field, the birth of a Sceptered Babe

Who rules without power and loves without restraint:

Our light, our hope, our path to lasting peace.

To all, on this Eve of Christmas,

Our love, our thanks and our sincerest wish

That you remember our gift of friendship

So we can share it for another year.

RE-SACRALIZING THE SACRED

One of my better students, who was enjoying a course I was teaching, asked me if I would like to speak to the members of his Bible study group. I felt honored and happily accepted his cordial invitation. The study group, comprised exclusively of young adults, met in the home of one of the students, an atmosphere most conducive to friendly discussions. I began my informal presentation by commending everyone present for taking the time and making the effort to study Sacred Scripture. The Bible, of course, I reminded them, has the great merit of being sacred. My eyes then fell upon a copy of a Sears' catalogue prominently displayed in a nearby bookcase, which, so I thought, would serve well in contrasting the sacred with the profane. My distinction, however, was immediately rebuffed. "That catalogue is sacred to my dad," piped one of the students. The group seemed to agree with my dissenter. How do I proceed, I thought to myself, if my audience was composed of relativists who have adopted the subjective view that things have value solely in relation to the individual and not in terms of the object itself? If nothing is sacred in itself, what is the point of studying Sacred Scripture? I did not disrespect the father's affection for his catalogue, but tried to explain that something is sacred not because we like it, but because it is sacred in itself. That distinction did not work any better. It was small consolation to me that the refreshments and light banter after my talk was mildly enjoyable.

I was familiar enough with how rampant relativism was among my students in general. It was trendy and appealed to their complacency. If everything is relative, then nothing is demanding. Relativism is a philosophy that makes for an easy life. Or so it seems. But I had hoped that things would be different with the study group. I should have known better. Professor Allan Bloom was right when he opened his best-seller, *The Closing of the American Mind* by saying, "There is one thing that a professor can be absolutely certain of: almost every student entering the university believes, or says he believes, that truth is relative." And if truth is relative, then so is the sacred. *Genesis* and the current issue of the Sears' catalogue stride together arm-in- arm. Equality reigns while moral perspicuity disappears.

The Bible is the Word of God. It is sacred because God is sacred. God is the Absolute and should not be relativized by the individual. If we are left with nothing more than the profane, how do we learn about the essential things of life: what we should believe, how we should live, and the reason for our coming into this world? John Updike spoke of his generation as existing "between the death and rebirth of the gods, when there is nothing to steer by but sex and stoicism and the stars." But this is steering without a compass, navigating without the North Star. The profane of itself can never attain the sacred. The lower cannot reach the higher. And that is why the Word of God was given to us from above.

It was once the policy of the United States Army that every military plane flying over water must carry a collapsible boat containing food rations and a copy of the Bible in a waterproof package. The justification for including the Good Book was that "spiritual equipment can be as important as food and drink is to save lives." There was no thought of omitting the Bible and providing a consumer catalogue or a copy of the *New York Times*. Perhaps an army pilot could have made a more convincing presentation than I to my Bible students.

The noted psychiatrist Karl Gustav Jung has informed us that among the many hundreds of patients he has treated, "Among those over 35, there has not been one whose problem in the last resort was not that of finding a religious outlook in life." Perhaps I should have made a date with my Bible students for a time in the future when he youngest member of the group was over 35. "The deepest definition of Youth is," as the philosopher Alfred North Whitehead has remarked, "Life as yet untouched by tragedy."

Catalogues and newspapers offer us very little assistance when it comes to life's important questions. Queen Victoria, upon losing her beloved husband confided that the Bible was her greatest source of comfort. And so it has been, for millions of people throughout history and throughout the world. The Bible is surely no ordinary book. Not only is it the most important and most widely read book ever written, but it is God's loving instruction to his wayward creatures. When we pray, we speak to God, when we read Scripture, God speaks to us.

There is a movement afoot to remove Gideon Bibles from hotel rooms.

While this is occurring, salacious material is made increasingly available through pay TV in those very same rooms. When the sacred is desacralized, it does not take its place alongside the profane; it becomes disreputable. The need is only too apparent in our secular world to re-sacralize the sacred. Perhaps it is better to state that we need to recognize the sacred character of that which is essentially sacred.

Other Titles by Dr. DeMarco

- *Abortion in Perspective*
- *Sex and the Illusion of Freedom*
- *Today's Family in Crisis*
- *The Anesthetic Society*
- *The Shape of Love*
- *The Incarnation in a Divided World*
- *In My Mother's Womb*
- *Hope for a World without Hope*
- *Chambers of the Heart*
- *How to Survive as a Catholic in a Parochial World*
- *Character in a Time of Crisis*
- *The Many Faces of Virtue*
- *Timely Thoughts for Timeless Catholics*
- *New Perspectives in Contraception*
- *The Integral Person in a Fractured World*
- *Patches of God-Light*
- *The Heart of Virtue*
- *Virtue's Alphabet from Amiability to Zeal*
- *Biotechnology and the Assault on Parenthood*
- *Architects of the Culture of Death*
- *Being Virtuous in a non-Virtuous World*
- *The Value of Life in a Culture of Death*
- *A Family Portfolio in Poetry and Prose*
- *How to Flourish in a Fallen World*
- *In Praise of Life*
- *How to Remain Sane in a World That Is Going Mad*
- *Ten Major Moral Mistakes and How They Are Destroying Society*
- *Poetry That Enters the Mind and Warms the Heart*
- *Footprints in the Sands of Time*
- *Why I Am Pro-Life and Not Politically Correct*
- *Notes from the Underground: Dialogue with a World in Disarray*
- *Apostles of the Culture of Life*

St. John Bosco's dream of the two pillars

Stella Maris

Made in the USA
Middletown, DE
29 November 2018